Etta F. Babbage

The Phat Boy's

18 Years on the St. Lawrence

Etta F. Babbage

The Phat Boy's
18 Years on the St. Lawrence

ISBN/EAN: 9783337209834

Printed in Europe, USA, Canada, Australia, Japan

Cover: Foto ©Lupo / pixelio.de

More available books at **www.hansebooks.com**

THE

"PHAT BOY'S"

18 Years on the St. Lawrence.

THE PEOPLE MET AND THE THINGS SEEN.

A * Guide * for * Tourists * And * Travelers.

ELEVENTH EDITION.   COPYRIGHTED, 1892.

ETTA F. BABBAGE, Publisher.

ROCHESTER, N. Y.:
DEMOCRAT AND CHRONICLE PRINT, 47 & 49 EAST MAIN STREET.
1892.

EDWARD F. BABBAGE.

Edward F. Babbage, for many years the publisher of this little book, was known to thousands of people both of the New and the Old World. He was better and more familiarly known as the "Phat Boy," a sobriquet which he gained from his ponderous size. He added to a striking personal appearance, a genial nature that won him friends wherever he went, and a fund of stories that made for him a reputation as a *ranconteur*.

Mr. Babbage was born at Oak Orchard Creek, Orleans county, March 20, 1840, and removed to Rochester with his parents when a child. In boyhood he and his twin brother, Dr. E. F. Babbage, resembled each other so strongly, that even intimate friends of the family were unable to distinguish between the two, and this close resemblance continued until they had nearly reached middle age. They were exactly of a height, and when young men, dressed in such a manner as to sustain the delusion. In later life, however, the subject of this sketch outstripped his brother in weight. At the time of his death he weighed 335 pounds.

When the Fifth Engineer Corps came home from the war, several of the survivors, who had helped to lighten the hours of camp life with song and joke, organized the "Pontoon Minstrels," and Mr. Babbage was sent out as advance agent. The company proved a success from the start, and for three years the minstrels traveled back and forth between Maine and California. Mr. Babbage was eminently successful as an advance agent, and the many experiences with which he met in the days when negro minstrelry was at the height of its popularity, furnished an unlimited source for the amusing stories he was wont to tell in after life. The company finally dissolved, its members retiring to business pursuits, and Mr. Babbage's services were sought for by the managers of nearly all the minstrel companies then on the road. He finally engaged with "Happy Cal" Wagner, who unwittingly bestowed upon him the nickname which he ever afterwards carried. Wagner sent a telegram to Babbage, who was then at his home in Rochester, and not knowing his initials, addressed it through an error of orthography "Phat Boy Babbage."

Mr. Babbage remained at the head of Wagner's company for several years, and afterwards represented in succession La Rue's Minstrels, McEvoy's Hibercon and Sam Hague's troupe. It was formerly his boast that there was not a town of 5,000 inhabitants in the United States which he had not visited.

After retiring from the theatrical business, Mr. Babbage was connected with the St. Lawrence Hotel in Montreal for a short time. He then entered the employ of the Grand Trunk railway and the Richelieu & Ontario Navigation Company, and conducted a ticket office at Niagara Falls for a year. In 1872 he was transferred by these companies to the excursion business along the St. Lawrence, and since that time had traveled up and down that river continuously during the summer. To travelers he was known as the "St. Lawrence guide." He represented the companies in the south during the winter, and had spent but little time at his home in Rochester for several years.

Mr. Babbage often referred facetiously to his superfluous flesh as having been the foundation of his business success.

Mr. Babbage died suddenly at the Marsden House, Alexandria Bay, June 23, 1891, having but recently arrived at the scene of his summer work. Death came as a sudden summons to the whole-souled genial man. He left one daughter, Etta F. Babbage, who bravely took up the work of her father and carried it on successfully for the summer of 1891, herself personally superintending the distribution of books and maps, and attending to other details of the business, at Cornwall Brothers' dock. Mr. Babbage was a member of the Odd Fellows and the Benevolent and Protective Order of Elks.

A CARD.

In assuming this work which my father conducted for the last eighteen years so successfully, I shall endeavor to continue it in harmony with his ideas and plans, which, by reason of our relationship, have long been familiar to me.

It is the only correct guide for the tourist or traveler down this delightful river of the Thousand Islands; a description of every point of interest suggested by the thousand and one questions asked of my father during his many years of service as "Guide to the St. Lawrence." It is a continuation also of the incidents described in the selections entitled: "The People I Have Met and the Things I Have Seen," which have served so well to entertain the traveler, and relieve somewhat the monotony incident to a work exclusively descriptive.

It is not my purpose to attempt any new description of the natural scenery of the Islands or the Rapids, but rather to describe, as occasion demands, the changes and improvements wrought by the hand of man.

In putting out this little volume I cannot ask for it a more cheerful greeting than it received during the life of him whose memory we cherish.

Very respectfully,
ETTA BABBAGE.

THE "PHAT BOY'S" HOTEL.

The "Phat Boy" issued the following prospectus for a hotel. He said that so long as the doors were made large enough to admit *him*, he did not care much whether the establishment was constructed in Ottawa or Utah, but for sundry and manifold reasons would prefer the latter locality. Here is the scheme, however, that he said that it would take a "Grœco-Roman" to wrestle with :

"PROSPECTUS."

This new hotel, to be called *The "Phat Boy's" Arms*, and to be built for the special comfort and convenience of travelers. On arrival every guest will be asked how he likes the situation, and if he says the hotel should have been placed on the knoll, or farther down towards any particular street, the location of the house will be immediately changed.

Corner front rooms, up one flight, for every guest.

Baths, gas, hot and cold water, laundry, telegraph, restaurant, fire alarm, bar-room, daily paper, sewing machine, grand piano, a clergyman and all other modern conveniences in every room.

Meals every minute if desired, and consequently no second table. English, French and German dictionaries furnished every guest, to make such a bill of fare as he may desire, without any regard to the bill affair afterwards in the office.

Waiters of any nationality or color desired. Every waiter furnished with a libretto button-hole bouquet, full dress suit, ball tablet, and his hair parted in the middle. Every guest will have the best seat in the dining hall, and the best waiter in the house. Any guest not getting his breakfast red hot, or experiencing a delay of sixteen seconds after giving his order for dinner, will please mention the fact at the office, and the cook and waiter will be blown from the mouth of a cannon in front of the hotel at once.

Children will be welcomed with delight, and are requested to bring hoops, and hockey sticks to bang the carved rosewood furniture, especially provided for that purpose, and peg tops to spin on velvet carpets. They will be allowed to bang on the piano at all hours, yell in the halls, slide down the banisters, fall down stairs, carry away dessert enough for a small family in their pockets at dinner, and make themselves as disagreeable as the fondest mother could desire. Washing to be allowed in rooms and ladies giving an order to " put on a flat iron," will be put on one any hour of the day or night.

A discreet waiter who belongs to the Masons, Odd Fellows and Knights of Pythias, and who was never known to even tell the time of day will be employed to carry milk punches and hot toddies, to ladies' rooms in the evening.

Every lady will be considered the belle of the house, and run boys will answer the belle promptly.

Should any run boy fail to appear at a guest's door with a pitcher of ice water, more towels, a gin cocktail and a pen, ink and paper before the guest's hand has left the bell knob, he will be branded 'Fraud' on the forehead and imprisoned for life.

The office clerk will be carefully selected to please everybody and can lead in prayer, play draw poker, match worsted at the village store, shake for the drinks any hour, day or night, play billiards, a good waltzer, can dance the German, make a fourth at euchre, amuse the children, and repeat the Beecher trial from memory, is a good judge of horses, and as a railway and steamboat reference, is far superior to Appleton's or any other guide, will flirt with any young lady, and will not mind being cut dead when " pa comes down," don't mind being damned any more than a Connecticut river, can room forty people in the best room in the house when the hotel is full, attend the annunciator, and answer questions in Greek, Hebrew, Choctaw, Irish, or any other polite language at the same moment without turning a hair.

Dogs allowed in any room in the house, including the w(h)ine room. Gentlemen can drink, smoke, chew, swear, gamble, stare at new arrivals, and indulge in any other innocent amusement, common to watering-places, in any part of the hotel.

The landlord will always be happy to hear that some other hotel is "the best house in the country."

Special attention given to parties who can give information as to "how these things are done in 'Yurrup'"

The proprietor will take it as a personal afront if any guest on leaving shall fail to dispute his bill, tell them that they are swindlers, their house a barn, their table wretched, their wines vile, and that he, at least, was never so imposed upon in his life.

THE "PHAT BOY'S" 18 YEARS
ON
THE ST. LAWRENCE RIVER.

THE St. Lawrence River, with its Thousand Islands and Rapids, is day by day attracting more and more attention among tourists. There is so much that is grand, weird, sublime and exhilarating in the scenery and balmy atmosphere of the majestic river, as it passes in its onward flow from the lake to the gulf, that we need not for a moment wonder why it is that there is a great annual increase in the number of those intelligent people, who, from East, West and South, repair to its placid waters in summer to recuperate their wasted energies and enjoy that luxuriating season known to every American as " vacation."

A vacation on the St. Lawrence means a sojourn at some pretentious or lowly cottage, or at some hotel of either class for a few days, or for one, two or more weeks, as the time, finances and inclinations of the individual may dictate ; or it may, as in hundreds of instances it does, only include a voyage of rapid transit from New York to Utica, Clayton, Niagara Falls, Lewiston, Toronto or Kingston to Alexandria Bay or Montreal, then return home. There are several different popular starting places to reach the river ; it is presumed you will take the most convenient one, and we will consider ourselves pleased with the selection.

HERE IS WHERE YOU BEGIN,

dear reader, to peruse an effort of mine which has taken up my leisure moments for the past eight months; it is not a physical effort, or it would have been larger, but being a literary one is a good reason why it can be held within such a small space as two hundred pages. A physical effort anywhere near my size you would have very little use for. While traveling, where could you store it away? No sardine box would hold it. You could not put it into a satchel or trunk nor tuck it away in any little convenient place. But this little volume can be carried most anywhere. I have tried to make it of such a desirable size that it can rest secure in the coat pocket, shawl-strap or in the hand. It is a dose for an adult, not to be shaken before taken, as you are expected to shake until your sides ache before you get through it; do not be in a hurry; take it easy, it is more pleasant that way. Do not feel offended if your name is not mentioned among "The People I Have Met." Think what a large head it would take to contain all I have passed through; but console yourself that you may be among "The Things I Have Seen."

It is a pleasure as well as a duty to state that I am indebted to Mr. George C. Hawley, Stenographer, of Rochester, N. Y., who so ably assisted me in taking my dictation for this work.

HOW THE METHODIST CHURCH LOST A BISHOP.

Some time ago, way back in the fifties, I had acquired a taste for reading, and purchased a copy of the New York Ledger, which was then publishing, for the first time, the story entitled "The Gun Maker of Moscow." My father, who was an ardent and vigorous Methodist, inquired what I was reading; I said the "New York Ledger;" he says, "What, story papers, novels?" "Why," I said, "I did not know, it was a paper published and it contains stories," and he remarked, "Do you like stories?" and I said, "Well, I have not as yet acquired much taste for stories. This is the first story that I ever attempted to read, except Robinson Crusoe and Jack, the Giant Killer. I read old Rob. until he found a companion named Friday, then I dropped him. So I cannot say that I have acquired much taste for story reading. However, I might develop that taste." So my father promised to buy a book with a story on every page if I would read it through. So, boy like, I promised I would, and he proceeded to purchase me a book, which I found after being presented, was a Bible, and as I had made my promise, I intended to keep it, but extorted from him another promise, that after I had read it through, that he would buy me another book, knowing that it would not be another Bible. I read it through; not understandingly, but because I desired to keep my promise to my father.

Handing him the Bible one day, I said, "There, father, I have read that book through, as I promised I would." He, smiling, said, "Can't you find any new stories in this? I have been reading this good book for over forty years and I can find a new story every time I open or peruse its blessed pages." "Well," I said to him, "you promised that when I had read this through you would buy me another book and I know you will keep your word," which he did, and the next book he bought for me was an edition of Spurgeon's

Sermons, which of course, was a change, and I perused it with great care together with pleasure as well as benefit.

One sermon in particular impressed me and that was one he preached to sailors going from England to Wales on board ship one Sunday when becalmed. It was simply a collection of fine stories, beautifully woven together, and as I had acquired a taste for story telling, it was very easy for me to commit the sermon to memory by using four or five little notes which could be placed upon a common calling card. It was the duty of our whole family to attend church at least three times of a Sunday and once on Sunday night, for we were always regular, but this Sunday night in particular, it did seem to me as if the heavens were open and we were to experience a second deluge, for I never in my life saw it rain so hard, and we were to be dragged out to church in that shower, quite a distance to the Swamp Angel Methodist Church, so I interposed a condition and stated that if father would stay at home, as well as the rest of the family, I would preach them a sermon. My father looked me straight in the eye and said, "Where did you get your sermon from?" and I said, "From the book you presented me," and he said, "All right ; we will stay at home." And so the family, at his call, went into the parlor and were seated. Afterwards I came in and placing the Bible on the centre-table, opened it to where my text was and placed a little card with the notes therein. After singing a hymn selected from the books we had, my father was requested to pray, which he did, and I arose to deliver myself of the discourse, which lasted one hour and ten minutes. My father's eyes were upon me from beginning to end, and while the tears rolled down his cheeks my attention was called to the furrows they had made in his face, and when I closed we sang another hymn and my mother closed the services with prayer.

The only thing religious that I forgot was the taking up of a collection and dismissing them with a benediction, but my mother told me the next day that my father never slept a wink that night, and the next morning placed $500.00 in the Rochester Savings Bank to my mother's credit, and went to see Professor Dewey to purchase a scholarship for me in the Rochester Theological Seminary, but the next day I ran off with a circus, and the next twenty years of my life I spent in the show business. So you see how close I came to becoming a bishop.

It is evident that nature done her part of it in giving me this manly form and ponderous size, therefore if I had done my part and went to college, there is no doubt that I would have forced myself to the front and become a Bishop.

MY VISIT AT THE SUNDAY SCHOOL EASTER.

I am not positive as to the day, whether Ash-Wednesday, Candlemas day, Patrick's day or Good Friday, it was one of those days that my twin brother, Dr. E. F. Babbage, said to me "Let us visit the church and Sunday school of our youth, that we attended 36 years ago, next Easter day." I accepted the invitation and joined him and proceeded to the Cornhill M. E. Church. We were greeted upon our arrival by our old friend, Brother George Leat, who escorted us to a front seat near the preacher, that we might drink in a sufficient quantity of the spirit at short range. The printed program which was distributed among the audience was rendered in a very pleasing manner, and the pastor preached an able sermon about charity and the beauty of giving to the cause of missions.

After the sermon we were invited to remain to Sunday school and were requested to take seats upon the platform with the superintendent during the session of the school. We were asked to make some remarks. The Doctor arose and in a few well chosen words informed the scholars that he was not much of a talker, but he had brought his little brother along who was a public speaker and who would be more than pleased to address them. Of all the embarrassing positions that it has been my good fortune to have been placed in, this was really the climax. I have in my life time addressed audiences ranging from 100 to five thousand, but never had spoken to an audience composed of children. Not until after I had risen to my feet did I take in the situation. It became self-evident to me that it required a sage philosopher to address a Sunday school and I knew that I was none, but it was necessary for me to say something, therefore I told them that 36 years ago I was a scholar, seated where these little boys were; that all of the religious instructions that I had ever received were imparted to me in this church and Sunday school; that for thirty odd years I had been thrown upon the world, and that the amount of spiritual teachings that I took in while a boy had sustained me through all these years, and I hoped for the next 30 years all of these little boys and girls within the hearing of my voice might expand and grow in good deeds to be as much better Christian men and women than I am larger than you are to-day.

IS IT COOL AND PLEASANT AT THE THOUSAND ISLANDS?

I am asked that question scores of times during the winter months, by people who are desirous of finding a comfortable place to rest during the heated term. After taking a perspective view of this huge mountain of flesh, the 330 lbs. which adorn my manly frame, they fire this question at me: "Do you pretend to say that the climate at the Thousand Islands is such that a person possessing the avoirdupois which you appear to have, can be made comfortable without the aid of a fan mill or a Wickes Refrigerator?" All that is necessary for me to say is, for 18 summers, I have made it my home as it is the only place I can recuperate my lost energy. If there is any device which will more accurately test the heat than a shirt collar of a man whose weight is 330 pounds, I would like to be in possession of it. I make the statement, and I am willing to prove it by a preponderance of evidence, that there has never been but two days in any summer that I have been overcome by heat, nor more than two nights but what this 330 pounds could slumber 9 hours under a blanket. Two nights last summer I will admit were uncomfortable. If the dear reader will pardon me, I will relate a little incident which befell me. One of these hot nights I awoke and found myself lying upon my back. The perspiration had oozed from my manly brow, filling the hollow of my eyes to such an extent that I could not open them. It dawned upon me that the best thing I could do would be to perform a contortion act and turn this large body over on its side so that the water might run out. I did so and the experiment proved a complete success.

MY ELEVENTH COMMANDMENT.

It has been my good fortune during life to have traveled a great many miles—been in every city in North America that has a population of ten thousand souls, and in some states have visited nearly every town and county. I have a natural inclination to observe not only men, but I have made a study of human nature, consequently I give it as my opinion that about eight out of every ten persons that I have had the pleasure to meet, have in his or her lifetime received religious instruction when young, have attended Sunday school more or less, and have been impressed with the ten commandments. Some no doubt have committed them to memory, and have abided by them and used them as a guide until they have attained the age of maturity or discretion. There are those possibly who have found it incumbent and necessary to add my eleventh commandment, which reads thus: "Thou shalt look after thyself first, last and all the time, and the green stuff." Many I have met who have discarded the ten commandments altogether and held the eleventh exclusively. Relating this little story regarding my codicil to the ten commandments, to a fellow passenger on board the steamer "Chicora," plying between Toronto and Lewistown, he informed me that they had an eleventh commandment in England, which he learned before he came to America which read thus; "Do up everybody or else everybody will do you up." A gentleman from the Green Isle perchanced to hear this and said, "Begorra, you want to add a little to that: 'And thou shalt not get caught at it.'" Now, dear reader, you can pay your money and take your choice.

"DON'T DO IT."

This startling head-line when it strikes the eye, denotes that there is something to be said of personal benefit to the reader of the article, and we hope to make it pleasant as well as profitable to those who take the time to peruse it. To begin with, we desire to say, don't get fat ; do not allow yourself to develop beyond the line which is laid down for the average man or woman ; because, if you do, the average chair will not fit, the average seat in a railroad coach will be too small ; you will be obliged to shrink into it, and then take up the seat of another after you get in. The same trouble will occur at amusements, which you enjoy very much, but it so distorts you to occupy the chair that the pleasure is lost : the average door to a hack is too small, and so is the omnibus, and you are obliged to walk. Here you will enjoy it, especially if it is a little slippery, dropping now and then three hundred and thirty pounds, because your friend thinks it does not hurt a fat man to fall. You will get little sympathy from anyone, this I guarantee, because I have tried it. By way of illustration, if I had not eaten anything for three days but a yard of pump water, and was to come to a friend and say I was hungry, and had not had anything to eat for three days, he would look me all over, and in reply would say: "Well, I guess you can stand it until next fall." So the fleshier you are, the less sympathy you get. And "If Dr. Tanner stood it for forty days, you have sufficient fat to last you six months, to say the least." Second, you become, as it were, a curiosity, and all look at you with amazement, and wonder what circus or side show you escaped from, or to what dime museum you belong. Third, there isn't anything made for the average man that will fit you, therefore everything must be made to order that you wear, except a necktie, pair of socks or handkerchief. The latter must be seven-eights of a yard wide in order to hold the perspiration it will mop up in once passing over your manly brow.

After you have become a little above the average size, as I have in development, and are conspicuous, everybody will know you ; if they do not, it will be easy for them to find out ; all they are obliged to do is to ask anyone. You will not know only those of your relations and friends very near to you. Then this world will be very lonesome and cold, or your experience will be different from mine. No one will ever ask you to "get in and take a ride," no matter what the circumstances may be—as they think of forty accidents that might occur, and you are too large a body for the average springs or seat in any vehicle. It would be a treat (were you not sensitive) if you could walk one block and hear the expressions that come from the vulgar throng as they pass. One female, with eyes like two saucers, exclaimed : "Glory be to the father, Mary Ann, phwat's that ?" And another says, "Gott in himmel, what a fat man," or a lady of color declare, "Umph! Umph!! Dat am de fattest man I ebber seed."

SIR WALTER PELHAM, ENGLAND'S GREATEST HUMORIST.

paid the Thousand Islands a visit, and gave his unique entertainments in different places. While in a conversation with him on the dock one day a steamboat arrived with about two hundred passengers on board and remained about fifteen minutes, during which time Mr. Pelham stood by my side taking in the situation. After the boat had left he remarked that it was a fortunate thing to me that I was not sensitive in regard to my personal appearance, etc. " For " said he, " of these two hundred passengers I do not believe one of them missed seeing you and scanning your manly form from head to foot. I would suggest that when you die you be placed in a memorial window for future generations to gaze upon." When he had finished these complimentary remarks I presented him a copy of my book. The next day a poem was handed me, together with Mr. Pelham's compliments, and I am sorry to say that it has been lost, strayed or stolen, and consequently I am unable to produce it in full, and can only give what little I remember.

From Florence to E. F. Babbage.

In your " People I have met and the Things that I have seen,"
I noticed you your widowerhood deplore ;
    Now, I am a slender maid,
    Not of adipose afraid,
Who could love you if you scaled a hundred more.

If you were twice your size, my sighs the same I'd breathe,
    Fat ne'er puts out a flame that's lit by love ;
    Then come along with me,
    And let us married be,
And be my little, popsie wopsie dove.

For when we two are one, the better half then I,
    Your adipose of course will half be mine,
    Therefore at once agree,
    Oh ! think how sad 'twill be,
Thy Fatima for you to longer pine.

Oh, guide of sweet St. Lawrence, devote your fat to Florence,
And leave the wandering river's flowing tide;
    The beauty of the waters
    Compare not with Eve's daughters,
So make me just the happiest of brides.

Then board the nuptial craft, or matrimonial raft,
Your oil will sure subdue life's stormy waves;
    And live with me in peace,
    And have your joys in grease,
Till called to lard our vaults or common graves.

"Till death do us part, as it were, etc."

A LITTLE ONE FOR THE BENEFIT OF "DANA'S" SUN.

George P. Ewing, a congenial drummer for a celebrated New York manufacturing company, chanced to hear a conversation between a mother and her daughter while taking a trip from Alexandria Bay to Montreal. The young lady had purchased a copy of my book, and after reading it had handed it to her mother, who, upon looking at the picture on the cover, exclaimed very excitedly, "Where did you get that fearful book with Grover Cleveland's picture on it?" The daughter soothed the old lady by telling her that it was not Cleveland's picture, but it was a photo of Mr. Babbage, and the book contained a description of the St. Lawrence River, written by the Author after Eighteen years' service, and a perusal of it gave her more pleasure than anything she had read since she left home.

A HORSE ON THE SCHOOL MARM.

The large verandas of the different hotels, cottages and houses of the Thousand Islanders, support easy rockers and comfortable furniture of all sorts for the accommodation of their guests, and when full and brought in close proximity, present fine opportunities to relate reminiscences and spin yarns until one cannot rest. I will say that I had the pleasure of being one of a lively crowd who had assembled on the balcony of one of the large hotels last summer; there were twenty of us, and all females with the exception of myself, and I am a female's friend. I soon found that I was in the midst of a lot of school teachers, and before I could recover my accustomed modesty, I was persuaded to relate a funny story; at first I declined with the explanation that I could not think of any story that would be of interest to them, but, I remarked, that as you insist upon my saying something, and as I observe that you are all school teachers, I will relate the school marm story. There was a little red school house in a very remote place; two boys were near a window looking out; one of the boys being much larger than the other, he saw in an adjoining lot a mule; turning to his schoolmate he said: " Johnnie, if I had a couple of lips like that mule, I would like to kiss the school marm." This caused the smaller boy to laugh, which attracted the school teacher's attention; she called him forward and interrogated him as to the cause of his laughter; he said he did not care to tell. " But if you do not I will whip you." He related in substance what his friend had said after much persuasion; as a punishment she kept the larger boy after school. One of the young ladies remarked, that if she had been that teacher she would have whipped him right on the spot, and I said, " no you wouldn't, you wouldn't hit a boy on the spot; that is the worst place in the world to strike a boy." She blushed, covered both hands with her face and I left.

MY MEETING WITH DAVID DUDLEY FIELD, OR HOW I EARNED TWENTY-TWO CENTS.

A season or two ago Alexandria Bay was honored with a visit from David Dudley Field, the distinguished jurist. Seeing one day he was about to be a passenger on the boat Island Wanderer for a trip among the Islands, I thought I would introduce myself to him, and at the same time make him a present of my book and map, as it would give him the name of every island, cottage and stopping place of the boat on her trip. Approaching him I said : "Mr. Field, I have here a little book which on page 49 commences a description of your trip this afternoon." He took the book (it was then called Humorous Lectures) out of my hand and upon reading the title said : " I don't want anything humorous ;" and I remarked that it was only humorous where it was not descriptive, and if he didn't care for it I had a picture of the St. Lawrence River. Before I could say any more he had turned the book over and saw the price of it was twenty-five cents, and he commenced going through almost a contortion of body, and fumbling in his pockets for the twenty-five cents to get rid of me, and I saw that his efforts were in vain, for all he could produce was twenty-two cents, and he forced me to take it, notwithstanding the fact that I had said to him that I came there for the purpose of making him a present of my book, also a picture of the St. Lawrence River, which I repeated again. Then he said, "Why didn't you do it then," and my answer was, that "You didn't give me time, and seeing that you have thrust this twenty-two cents upon me I shall have the pleasure o keeping it until I return home, and then it shall go into my museum of curiosities. When you come and visit me you shall see it."

HOW WOMEN FISH.

Having read various descriptions of how fishing is carried on by the fair sex at the several watering places, permit us to mention some of them. One writer said : "Ah ! what joy to have a bite ; what rare delight to find one's bait gone "—and it was only by the suicidal policy of some water-weary fish who chanced to pass our way that we could record one fish for our day's sport. How different is the fishing at the Bay.

As an illustration, a very funny anecdote was recited to me by Mr. J. C. Colvert, editor of the Cleveland *Leader*, who said, " Talk about ladies catching fish ; I am somewhat of an angler myself and take a great deal of comfort fishing at the Bay. The other day I was out fishing with my wife, who, by the way, had no pretensions as a captivator of the finny tribe, yet she caught seven fish before I had time to put my line into the water." This somewhat astonished me, and I remarked that he must have been very slow that morning. He answered by telling me, " No ! On the contrary, I was very lively ; all my time was employed taking the fish off and baiting her hook." He entered a protest after that and let the boatman attend to Mrs. Covert's line while he enjoyed the sport.

A gentleman says of the fishing near the Hudson : " The first thing a woman does when she goes fishing is to make herself look as hideous as possible—a sort of a cross between the Witch of Endor and Meg Merrilies. This is done by a hideous straw hat big enough to cover a chicken coop, the oldest and most unbecoming dress she has got, a pair of gloves six sizes too large, and, if possible, rubber boots. And the sight of woman, lovely woman, so dressed, presents a spectacle of pity." You will not have occasion to pity any of the ladies, who go fishing from the Bay, for they look so jaunty you would envy them and their enjoyment as well as fish. I have known Mrs. Madden and party to bring home thirty fish varying in size from a 3¼ black bass to a 7 pound pickerel. A friend writes from C—— Lake, telling how he spent a day fishing there, accompanied by three ladies and a gentleman friend. "Women never step into a boat here, they always jump. Of course she slips, falls down, yells for help, nearly upsets the boat, and is put to rights by the most eligible young man in the party. Nothing will do then, but she must row, and she knows as much about rowing as a cow does about billiards. She handles her oars as if they were trees, splashes every one with water, and after half an hour's work she is about ten feet away in the wrong direction, when one of the men takes the oars and we are soon at our fishing place. She tries to bait her hook, and after getting the hook into all her fingers (in fact everywhere but into the minnow), her friend baits her hook, and she throws it out. The first time it catches onto one of the ladies' ears, the next throw into the back of the gentleman's neck, and the third time into the coat of her friend, who quietly cuts it out (it is his best coat), and he gently puts the line into the water without saying a cuss word, and says he hopes she will catch a whale.

After a few moments of quiet all are informed she has a bite ; she pulls it in steadily to find it is part of the carcass of a dead horse. She is soon relieved of the burden and catches a small perch. She is so delighted that she must let it flop into the faces of every one in the boat, tries for twenty minutes to take it off the hook, but her fingers are so sore she lets the job out to her male companion. One of the other ladies has sat for two hours without moving a muscle, while the other I believe, would fish with a hair-pin baited with a piece of red flannel, hung to a skein of silk in a stationary wash-tub, and solemnly declare when she got through that she had millions of bites. Dear lady readers, we have no such experiences to relate at Alexandria Bay. The boats are the prettiest, the fishermen the nicest, the fish the largest and best, the boatman bait your hooks. The hotel furnishes the lunch, and you are sure to catch fish. When they are cooked and you eat your meal served upon an Island, and do not say you have had the most pleasant day ever spent fishing, draw on me for the balance. P. B.

A WORD TO MY PROFESSIONAL FRIENDS.

While it may not be known to all who are fortunate enough to obtain a copy of my work and peruse the same, nevertheless it is a fact that about twenty years of my life I was engaged in what is commonly called the show business.

In 1858, I started in, in the employ of Mr. George Lee of New York City, now proprietor of Port Jarvis, N. Y., Opera House, in connection with Jack Hudson and Billy Jackson, who were considered at that time the best side show people in the business. I then connected

myself with John Graffam as a glass blower in 1860 and
'61. My next step was with the Woodruff Bros., later
George Woodruff, the celebrated Bohemian troop of
fancy glass blowers, La Rue's Carnival Minstrels, and
MacEvoy's Hibernicon, etc., etc. It would be a pleasure
to go on and write a detail sketch of my career as a
showman, but the old saying is, that life is short and we
have not long to live and we are certainly a long time
dead. I will omit a biographical outline of my life until
later; I will say that it has been a pleasure to me to
meet my old associates and professional friends during
my 18 years on the St. Lawrence, among which I am
pleased to mention Mr. Sol Smith Russell, whom I first
met as far back as 1867. He was quite young at that
time, but full of ambition and talent, and I have watched
with a great deal of interest his professional career. I
have many a little anecdote which I could relate of his
ability, tact and humor, but it is a question in my mind
whether they would be of interest to my readers, and I
know not whether Mr. R. would love to have them published. I will be brief and say, that had I been a wise
man I would have accepted the position offered me to
become his manager, which he proffered. I would have
been worth a half million instead of Mr. Fred D. Burger
his present courteous and amiable manager who can
draw his check for that amount. I do not envy them,
am only glad to be classed with their " Poor Relations."
Ed. Harrigan and his manager, Mart W. Hanley, with
their families, made the trip with me from Niagara
Falls to Montreal, taking the steamer from Kingston
through the Thousand Islands and Rapids of the St.
Lawrence to Montreal. After watching Mr. Harrigan
all day, and noticing how minutely he takes in all that

surrounds him, and how for hours he was among the deck hands studying character, I am satisfied how easy it must be for him to write a play depicting the many positions and scenes in every day life that he has himself passed through. I called upon him in May and found the two young kids Johnnie Wild and Billy West with Reilly and the four hundred. Wm. R. Hayden, Senator Crane, Vokes Family, Jno. P. Smith, W. S. Meysteer, Mr. and Mrs. Chas. MacEvoy, Mr. Neil Burgess, Henry E. Abbey, John Schœffel, Lafe Heidel, John Henshaw, Frank B. Cilley, Charles B. Ghrist, Gus Williams, Dan Morris Sullivan and Mr. Joseph Murphy, Tom Karl, the great Barnaby, P. T. Barnum, Buffalo Bill, Denman Thompson, Charles J. Evans, Gus Pennoyer, Frank Edwards, Charles H. Bradshaw, Pierce Jarvis, E. O. Rogers, Mr. James Lewis, John W. Ransone and wife, and enough others to more than half fill the soup tureen.

THE- ONE I ENVIED MOST.

A short time ago a party of old-time show people perchanced to assemble in one of the leading hotels in Rochester. It was my pleasure to be among the number. After listening to a large amount of old narratives of trial and tribulation I was called upon to delineate one. I did so and the substance of it I will state here in a narrative form for the benefit of some young aspirant who desires to follow the business.

Gus Pennoyer, the agent, business manager and treasurer of the great actress, Lotta, and myself were doing the Pacific coast in 1872. I was the accredited representative of Charles MacEvoy's original Hibernicon. We had been in San Francisco five weeks together. He started out one week ahead of me to bill Vallejo, Oakland, San Jose, Sacramento, Marysville, etc. As I followed him it was necessary in order to make my announcements of the coming of my show to cover his paper; on several occasions he very kindly allowed me to do so two or three days in advance. One day while at Marysville we went into the office of the hotel. I told him that I had a little matter that I wished to communicate to him and if he would take a seat I would divulge it. He did so and listened to me with a great deal of interest. I told him that as the agent and representative of Charles MacEvoy's Hibernicon I envied him and his position as agent of Lotta. He remarked laughing, "Well, hold on a minute, let us compare notes and so see who has got the best of it. What are your duties? What services do you render?" I said "I am his credited agent, and as such I secure all dates, lay out the routes, order all printing, and do all of the business connected with the success of the entertainment except giving the same. He follows in my track, pays all bills contracted by me." He asked me if it wasn't necessary for me to be with my company. I told him no I didn't see them sometimes for six weeks. I was always supplied with funds in advance by my manager. Then he said, "My dear boy, you have envied me and have been honest and told me of it. I am going to be honest and tell you that while I am the agent of Lotta my duties are very much different from yours. I have in charge Miss Lotta, her mother, a parrot and a dog, must attend to their transportation from place to place, and from depot to hotel, and from hotel to opera house or hall; must see that they have a corner front room on the parlor floor, must be ready at all times to match worsted at the corner grocery store, walk three or four miles per day to exercise the dog, sleep with one eye open to be ready to go for a doctor in case the old lady or the parrot should be taken ill, attend to the box office receipts as well as the tickets at the door, commit all the parts so as to be able to assume any one of the characters in the cast in case of sickness or inability to perform of some member of the troupe. You say you now have six hundred dollars of MacEvoy's money. I represent Lotta and don't carry five cents. Your salary is ten dollars a week more than mine. Taking everything into consideration I am of the opinion that you are the one to be envied, and not you to envy me.

YOU KNOW HER.

She is one of the strong minded of the female sex and generally has her own way in everything. At any rate, she stands ready at any and all times to combat with any one of the lords of creation, or otherwise, who may dispute her sway. We prefer your imagination to fill in a description, because it would be next to an impossibility for me to do so. She has all the requisites; the thin, tall figure, the hatchet face, sharp nose, wears glasses, and always carries an umbrella. About one each day will pass down this route in Summer, except when an Eastern or Western Excursion comes; then it will be hard to select those who are not of her kind. The first object that strikes her eye is our manly figure. After looking it well over, she remembers that fat people are proverbially jolly and good natured, so she breaks into conversation, and about the first question she asks is: "Were you always as large as you are now?" "Oh, yes! I was born this size." The answer causes her to discover that she has left out the word "proportion." So she apologizes, smiles for the first time, and we are friends for the trip.

WILL HE HAVE IT THERE?

An English tourist registered at "The Crossmon, Alexandria Bay, asked the clerk for a corner room up one flight, on shady side, a special hall boy, meals served in room, a bath, and candle instead of gas, steam heat and— "Hold on!" said the clerk; "I think you have made a mistake; this is not heaven."

LORD H. U. MERRIAM

was a visitor at Alexandria Bay one season, and while he remained put up, from choice, at the Marsden House, Alexandria Bay. We were very intimate and social during his stay, and I inferred he came where I take my meals to see if he could get as fat as I am.

WHAT I KNOW ABOUT ELI PERKINS.

Some few years ago Mr. Perkins was a Passenger on one of the boats. I do not know whether he took me for the captain, director or manager of the line, or not, but he exerted himself considerably to form my acquaintance. There was nothing unusual about that, however, as there is something "*distingue*" about me, and when on the boat I stand considerably "above proof." I have frequently dined at the same table with the Governor-General, Lord Dufferin, and retinue— after his lordship had left. But to return to Eli. The day in question I was upon the boat, as usual, describing the points of interest, especially the one on the Canadian shore, where the St. Regis Indians come year after year to gather the famous elm and basswood with which to make their celebrated baskets. I was delineating at some length upon the noble red man, when Eli came to me and said, "I will write you a verse of poetry about that." Glad to get a memento in that shape from so distinguished an individual, who had so often been accused of being witty, I said it would please me very much. Here is the verse:

> " Once here the noble red man took his delights,
>   Fit, fished and bled ;
>   Now most of the inhabitants are white,
>   With nary a red."

I thanked him very profusely, and on subsequent occasions took great delight in repeating the lines to the passengers, never forgetting for a moment to remind them that they were written for me by the alleged American humorist. One day, after delivering myself of the poetry and repeating to the passengers that it was written by the celebrated poet, writer, humorist and lecturer, Eli Perkins, I was approached by an exceedingly polite and affable gentleman, whom I learned was Mr. John H. Rochester, of Rochester, N. Y., who asked me if he understood me correctly in attributing the authorship of the lines quoted to Mr. Perkins. I assured him that he had written them expressly for me, and produced in Eli's own hand-writing the original copy. With a subdued smile resting upon his countenance, Mr. Rochester informed me that there must be an error somewhere, as a gentleman, a Mr. Fletcher, had written a poem in 1834, in which the exact verse occurred, and he proceeded to repeat the verse from memory. This took me slightly back, and I subsequently came to the conclusion, with "my friend" of the *Oil City Derrick*, that a cabbage leaf was never more at home than when in the crown of "Uli Perkins' hat." After that I had no more use for the poem, but determined if I ever met "Uli" I should call to his mind the circumstances connected with "his little poem." I had not long to wait, for one day, while in Evansville, Ind., at the St. George Hotel, I met the gentleman, and recalled the circumstances connected with the little verse, and he, with a perfect air of *nonchalance*, said that he had never given it a thought since—dashed it off in a minute. I told him how remarkable it was that great minds often run in the same channel, and related my experience with his gem. He scowled, and turning on his heel, said it was indeed a singular word-for-word resemblance, but changed the subject at once, and asked me to his room on the following morning, which invitation I cheerfully accepted, doting all the evening upon having a nice time, and swapping a few gags, etc., etc.; but my hopes were blighted, for the next morning I was informed of his very early departure—gone up to lie to the people of Rockport, I was told. "Uli" is a great man and contracts a larger amount of business upon a small amount of capital than any public character I know of. When Eli reads this I expect he will load his big gun—not intellectual, but otherwise—and come for me. I will therefore give him a pointer in advance; there won't anything scare me but a stomach pump.

H. R. CLARK, of New York.

This litte volume would not be complete if it did not mention his name, not only in connection with the fishing at Alexandria Bay, but the facts of his having given more time and money towards stopping illegal fishing than all the owners of cottages and islands combined. He was elected an honorable member of the Canadian Fisheries Commission, and was the prime mover in forming the Anglers' Association of the Thousand Islands, and personally captured more nets than all others interested. He is the most enthusiastic, as well as the best posted gentleman that comes to the Islands to fish, and knows more about the habits and nature of the finny tribe than any other party who comes here. He won the gold medal given for the largest and best catch of fish for the season of 1885. His standing offer to catch ten pounds of fish in a given hour, in any day, from the St. Lawrence River, during the season, or give ten dollars to any charitable institution I may mention, if he fails. Here is one of his catches on an eight-ounce rod, a single leader, a "G" line, a fish weighing seventy-eight pounds, girt measure twenty-nine inches, length sixty-three inches, time in landing one hour and five minutes. Beat this and I will tell you more.

Hon. A. CORNWALL, of Alexandria Bay.

Cornwall & Walton were the original purchasers of the Thousand Islands, in the American channel of the river, from the government. Mr. A. Cornwall is the survivor of the firm and therefore the father of them, and I call him Pa. If you desire any information not in this volume, call on him at the old stone stores of Cornwall Brothers, and he will give it to you cheerfully. He is an Encyclopedia of facts on the St. Lawrence or the Thousand Islands.

WHAT AND WHO MADE ALEXANDRIA BAY.

In 1872 President U. S. Grant visited this delightful spot, a guest of Geo. M. Pullman, of palace car fame, Pullman Island. There was at that time inadequate hotel accommodations, for the tourist as well as the visitor who had been drawn to this, the most beautiful, natural scenery in the world. Messrs. Cornwall and Walton, of Alexandria Bay, with their usual display of sense and sagacity, as well as business tact, for which they have always been commended, offered to give the best site on the St Lawrence to any man who would erect upon it a first-class summer hotel. Mr. O. G. Staples, of Watertown, N. Y., hearing of this offer came, he saw, and how he conquered you shall know as we proceed with our narrative. Well, he concluded to father the scheme. Securing a man with money, a Mr. Nott, of Syracuse, the ground, or rock rather, was broken January 14th, 1873, and the Thousand Island House was completed and opened July 17th, 1873, just six months from the day of starting. Rumor says that although their money gave out a little above the first story, Staples' indomitable will saw it completed and furnished, ready to receive guests, just as soon and as well as if he had been a millionaire. During the next two years of the partnership of Staples and Nott, everything did not go as smooth as a marriage bell, but still they went, and in the end Staples had the money and hotel. (I hope the reader, if he knows Staples, will not be so unkind as to accuse him of parting with all his experience and make the pun that he took the money and Nott the experience). Staples bought out Nott, and, I believe paid him what was agreed, and he run the hotel until April 15th, 1883, when Mr. R. H. Southgate (the man of many hotels, too numerous to mention here) bought him out. The many changes that have been made, and those contemplated, when completed, will make this the Mecca of summer resort watering-places, the Venice of America. I desire to say right here that I hope Mr. Southgate will not lose sight of what has in the past made the Bay popular as a resort. I like to see the standard of visitors raised as well as prices. I would like it to be the place for fish as well as those who love the piscatorial art. No dust, no dampness, no malaria or hay fever, no musquitoes ; light, dry air, cool and bracing. Thermometer never over 80 or below 50 in July or August, and one can enjoy what is denied them almost everywhere else, a good nine hours of cool refreshing sleep under a blanket. Those troubled with pulmonary complaints will find great relief here. Steamers, steam yachts and sailing vessels abound, everything to animate the scene and enhance the pleasure of visitors is done. Fishing, fishing boats, bathing, etc., as well as fish abound, and we say here, if you have never been to the Bay, come.

MY VISIT TO THE STATE FISH HATCHERY AT MUMFORD, NEW YORK.

Mr. Monroe A. Green, the superintendent of the State Fish Hatchery, gave me a very kind invitation to visit him and the State Hatchery, at the opening of the season, April 1st, 1890, which invitation I accepted (the same was extended for this year, but I was unable to accept). The event will always remain GREEN in my memory for it was indeed a glorious trip. Mr. Lapey, the Assistant General Passenger Agent of the Buffalo, Rochester & Pittsburgh Railway, issued transportation for myself and stenographer over his road from Rochester to Mumford and return. While on my way to the depot on the morning of my departure, I was greeted by a friend who inquired as to where I was going so early in the morning. I informed him that I was about to visit the fish hatchery at Mumford. He then, with premeditation and malice aforethought, asked me if I was going to spawn. I replied, "No, but to see them manufacture fish." Arriving at the depot at 7 o'clock and 30 minutes, we boarded the train and started. A friend invited me to sit in the smoker; but as I had just received my morning rations, and knowing that the fumes of the smoking car would have the tendency to force me to relinquish my grip on that meal, I declined his invitation and seated myself in the ladies' car. Arriving at Mumford we were met by a messenger and driven to the celebrated hatchery. Upon entering the main building we were received by Superintendent Green and his son Frank. We also met the following gentlemen who were on hand to try their luck in capturing the finny tribe; Mr. Wm. S. Kimball, Dr. Hurd, Mr. Samuel Wilder, Mr. C. C. Morse, Mr. Thomas Harris, of Rochester, and Mr. R. S. Coleman, of Sandy Hill, Washington Co., N. Y. The above named gentlemen were equipped with the necessary credentials and started out. Mr. Wilder was the champion of the day's fishing, having caught at least fifty good sized speckled trout. But if his friend "Bowman" had been there he would have doubled the number. Myself and stenographer remained at the large hatchery to receive information regarding the manufacture of fish. Superintendent Green has been interested in fish hatching 23 years and has the last few years hatched ten million fry per year, which are sent to nearly every county in the state. Ninety-five per cent of the fish that are hatched under his supervision live. The largest number of fish are hatched during the months of November and December. The Salmon Trout seem to be in the greatest demand, although German Trout are becoming very popular. Mr. Green has raised six hundred thousand German Trout since receiving forty thousand eggs six years ago. There are five districts in the state all supplied from the Mumford hatchery. It requires from two hundred to two hundred and fifty pounds of hashed liver to feed the fish daily. While we were receiving the above information a large gong sounded, which denoted the fact that Assistant Walzer had prepared a fine spread in an adjoining building. Seating ourselves at the table the fleshy man was requested to ask a blessing. He replied that the best he could do would be to recite the dude's blessing, which he did (a copy of which will be mailed to any one on receipt of a two cent stamp), and the party with a good will as well as a good appetite, did the subject ample justice. The next excitement was the catching of a two pound California Trout by the tail, and landing the same in 26 minutes, which act was accomplished by the short hand man with an 8 oz. rod. Thermometer, 4 degrees below freezo; pulse, 115; eyesight good.

THE LARGE GATHERINGS.

Round Island Park, Thousand Island Park and Alexandria Bay have, at different times, been honored by conventions, meetings of associations in convention, pilgrimages, etc., a minute description of which would fill a volume ten times the size of this one, so I can only mention what is uppermost in my mind, the Press Association of Vermont, under the guidance of S. W. Cummings, Esq., the general passenger agent of the Central Vermont Railroad. He and his associate, Mr. T. H. Hanley, made for them an ever to be remembered excursion trip. The Librarians of America stayed in the midst of the Thousand Islands three or four days. They were, without exaggeration, the most refined and educated body of men and women that I ever met. The Brooklyn Tabernacle, with its thousand pilgrims, were also delighted with everything they saw at the Thousand Islands, and were profuse in their expressions of its scenic beauty. I met the Rev. Dr. Talmage and had a personal interview. I don't wonder now that his magnetism holds such sway with his Brooklyn audience, and that the whole world receives so cheerfully through the telegraph his sermons.

THEY DO IT EVERY TIME.

When the average American's postage stamp does not stick he storms around and makes the air fairly blue until he secures the mucilage bottle and fixes the stamp to his letter. Not so with the average Canadian. He procures a needle and thread, sits quietly down and sews the darned thing on.

THE HUMORISTS OF AMERICA.

Most of these jovial, good-natured souls have, at some time or other, paid the Thousand Islands and the St. Lawrence River a visit, but it would be useless for me to try and remember each and every one of them, and their peculiarities. I cheerfully remember Mark Twain (Samuel L. Clemens, Esq.), and one of the funniest stories I tell was of an evening spent at Toronto, while a guest of a friend, and the little speech that he made introducing Senator Hawley, who was to make a political address at Elmira, N. Y. He was a passenger down the river. After naming over several towns and streets in the Province of Quebec, he remarked: "Are they all saints here ; no sinners?"

SALISBURY

of the *Fall River Advance*, going down the St. Lawrence, as a passenger, and his written description of the trip, is the most humorous that I have had the pleasure of perusing. "*Bob*" Burdette's of the *Burlington Hawkeye*, description of the Victoria Bridge is very funny. Knox, of the *Texas Siftings*, went down on the opposition line, so did not have a chance to meet him. Eli Perkins you cheerfully remember, and I have given a very definite description of an interview, in another part of this work.

REPRESENTATIVE MEN

of New York, New Orleans, Rochester, Buffalo, Pittsburgh, Cleveland and Chicago, respectively who occupy cottages, etc., at the Thousand Islands during the summer, should be mentioned here, but space alone prevents. This little volume is published expressly for

Tourists who travel, and if it becomes large, burdensome or cumbersome, it is useless for what it is designed, as a descriptive book of the St. Lawrence River. I therefore cannot lose sight of this fact, and must content myself with publishing a book that will contain about 180 or 200 pages.

H. H. Warner, of Rochester, N. Y.; George M. Pullman, Chicago ; N. H. Hunt, of Brooklyn, N. Y.; Royal H. Pullman, Baltimore, Md; C. B. Marsh, Chicago, Ill.; Judge Donahue, New York ; Rev. W. Dempster Chase, New York ; H. C. Wilber, Pres. Lehigh Valley R. R.; Rev. Dr. Saxe, Rochester, N. Y.; Fred W. Hawley, Rochester, N. Y.; C. H. & W. B. Hayden, of Columbus, O.; Judge Spencer, New York ; W. J. Lewis, H. A. Laughlin, G. T. Rafferty, J. S. Laney, of Pittsburgh ; J. C. Covert, the present Mayor Rose and Mr. J. M. Curtis, of Cleveland, Ohio ; Judge La Batte, New Orleans ; C. J. Henderson, of New York ; Judge Thomas Troy, of Brooklyn ; Hon. R. A. Livingston, N. Y.; M. B. Bettman, of New York ; John Lowery, of New York; E. & T. H. Anthony, Mr. J. W. White, of White Plains; H. R. Clark and family, of Jersey City ; Royal E. Deane, of New York ; last but not least, my solid friend, Col. T. G. Carnes, of Gainsville, Texas, a man after my own heart and weight as well. He says he enjoys himself more at Alexandria Bay, and can keep his three hundred and ten pounds cooler, than at any other resort in America, and when you are about to select a summer home think of me and my three hundred and thirty-three pounds, and after passing eighteen years on the St. Lawrence, I have not seen over two days in any summer that would cause me, through heat, to change my summer home.

THE PEOPLE WE MEET AT THE THOUSAND ISLANDS.

Visitors going to the the Thousand Islands will strike the river either at Kingston, Cape Vincent, Gananoqua or Clayton. The first of the summer resorts after leaving Clayton, is Round Island, which is occupied by the Baptists. The Hotel has been enlarged, refitted and refurnished and the name changed to Hotel Frontenac, under the management of Mr. Almy of New York, a hotel man of note and ability, but the denominational sectarian barriers have been removed the same as at each of the other resorts, and all Christians, of whatever sect, or no sect, are welcome. Even the dude can revel in his peculiarity. The next point is Grennell's Island Park where is located a very nice hotel and a number of fine cottages. Beyond is Thousand Island Park. This is occupied by the Methodists, and they welcome everyone, except on Sundays, when no persons are allowed to land on the island.

The Fine View House, Central Park and Edgewood Park have no religious proclivities known to me, but "Solomon Isaacs" would not be admitted at Edgewood Park unless he would swear that he was a "Quaker."

Westmister Park was founded by the Presbyterians, and is occupied by them and their friends. Summerland by the Universalists and their friends.

Alexandria Bay is cosmopolitan, where everybody is welcome and can stay as long as they behave themselves and pay their board.

Now, dear reader, imagine the Baptists, Methodists, Presbyterians, Universalists and all their friends combined, and now if you want a summer of pleasure without any baneful influences, you wouldn't miss it in securing the Thousand Islands for your summer home, where there are no bad people whatever, such as drunkards, loafers, tramps, people of bad repute, male or female, and if they should drift in they would receive a cool reception among the people of the Thousand Islands. It would not require a Pinkerton or any other detective to select from among those Christian people or their friends any bad character, but they come, nevertheless, though their stay is short.

CREDIT TO WHOM CREDIT IS DUE.

While we have spoken very pleasantly of the episode of H. H. Warner and George M. Pullman ; of their returning to their respective islands and expending nearly half a million dollars in beautifying them, after wandering from one end of the world almost to the other in search of comfort, proving conclusively that we have the finest watering place in America or we could not retain such men as these, I must say a few words in justice to those who remained with us during their absence ; who bore the burden and heat of the day and lavishly spent their money in fitting up their islands to make the Thousand Islands what they now are. Among those people I will mention A. B. Pullman, C. B. Marsh, N. H. Hunt of Brooklyn, N. Y., H. R. Heath, Royal E. Dean, E. W. Dewey, C. H. and W. B. Hayden, J. H. Oliphant, A. C. Beckwith, A. E. Clark, H. A. Laughlin, C. E. Hill, Hon. W. G. Rose, Mayor of Cleveland, O., J. M. Curtis and a host of others.

THE WHY NOT!

I am asked almost every day why the Canadians do not occupy the Islands in their channel of the river the same as the Americans do. The only answer I can give is, that the American comes here to rough it, fish and enjoy himself during the summer vacation, and the Canadians have it rough enough the year round, so do not have to come.

BOYS ON A STEAMER.

Here is a genuine. His parents are with him; he cannot keep still; he wants chiefly to break his neck or fall overboard, or to get crushed by the walking-beam; he has been twice dragged from the steps leading to the walking-beam used by the assistant engineer for lubricating purposes; he would like to get in the paddle boxes, has talked every officer on board to death, and is now trying his best to worry the deck hands. How curiously constructed is a real boy, to go whither he should not, and especially where his anxious mother most fears he will go; he is now doing his best to spoil his parent's trip. We can leave him for a moment; he won't flag in his endeavor to get into trouble or to make his parents miserable.

This is a smaller boy—not yet out of his petticoats, but very active; he, too, has with him an anxious mother; he has found another boy—a strange boy, of the same size and sex; they have become acquainted; the strange boy is allowed by his parents to roam about the boat at will; he invites the nice little boy to roam also; he wants him to roam as near the walking-beam as possible; he has roamed there before himself and

escaped ; he tells the nice little boy how cunning it is to
come near being crushed ; the nice little boy's mother
forbids any roaming at all ; she looks with disfavor on
the strange boy ; but the strange boy continues to hang
around ; he knows, so does the nice boy, together they
can fool any one mother ; united they stand, divided
they fall ; now the nice boy edges away from the side
of his mother, for her energies are momentarily concentrated on the set of her bonnet and the nice looking
gentleman at the other end of the saloon, who is taking
side glances at her through the mirror. Now the nice
boy gets farther away ; they are on a forbidden part of
the deck near the walking-beam. It is great fun. Now
the cross man who keeps order on the deck drives them
away. They go to the News agent's stand and help
themselves to anything on the table when he is not
looking. They are now running in and out the state
rooms, where the passengers have gone to take a little
rest, getting in everybody's way ; it is a wonder they
haven't been killed twenty times. It is great fun for the
boys, but almost death to the passengers. And the
mother is still so occupied with her bonnet and the
dude who has made a mash or favorable impression
upon her that she has not missed her nice little boy.

SIR JOHN A. McDONALD,

who is Canada's prime minister, has been a passenger
upon the boats, two and three times during each season,
until his face became a very familiar one to me, and I
must say that it is as jolly looking as my own, and
about as expressive ; while his is a Roman nose mine
is a pug. I remember his first trip down, after his
election to the premiership, and my saying to him :

"Now we ha.e a change in politics and in government, I shall expect of course, a position under the new government." Sir John A. remarked: "Yes, you shall have it. I shall make a change. We will have the rivers run the other way so you can be utilized day and night to make it pleasant for the people without extra pay or allowance." When giving my description of Barnhart's Island and the Canadian Channel passing around, the settlement of the treaty of 1812, and the ratification of the same by Lord Ashburton and Daniel Webster, he asked me if those were facts and I said, "Yes, and I am astonished to think that you would have to ask me about such an important point and treaty." When nearing Montreal I had finished giving a description of places and points of interest, and had described Bonsecours market when he told me that an Irish friend of his pronounced it different, he called it "Bone Scowered market."

WHAT I TOOK HEED OF.

Having been away from my native city, Rochester, for at least a year and a half, crossing the continent from the rock bound coast of Maine to the jumping off place in Florida, visiting nearly every city in this country, when I returned home I met my venerable pastor and beloved friend, the Rev. Dr. J. B. Shaw.

This gentleman always took a good deal of interest in my personal welfare and would warmly shake me by the hand whenever we would meet. He would interrogate me as to my prosperity and adversity. On this particular occasion he asked me where I had been; and after answering his questions to his entire satisfaction he noticed prominent upon my expansive shirt front my pin. After looking at it a moment he said, " Mr. Babbage, is that a diamond?" I replied in the affirmative. He remarked, " of the first water?" I replied, "yes, boiled in oil." He said, "that must represent a small house and lot." I said, "yes, sir, very nearly." He said, " why don't you sell that and give the money to the poor?" In answer I remarked, " while I wear it at your suggestion, I may part with it if you desire to have me." He said, " did I ever tell you to wear a diamond?" " No, not exactly ; but in a sermon you preached one Sunday you remarked that some of your friends had bright spots about them, others had none ; some the only one you could discover was a diamond they wore in their shirt front, so I went home and looked myself over in vain to find that bright spot, so I purchased this one. Does it fit me?" Laughingly he said, "do you treasure up everything that I say as faithfully as you did this?" I replied that I hoped that I did. He asked me if I was going to publish an edition of my book this year. I told him that I was about to issue another edition and that I had a copy of last year's book with me. I asked him if he would kindly accept a copy and read it, and to give me his opinion of it the next time I met him. He replied that he would. In about three weeks I met him and asked for his opinion. He smiled and remarked that it was a very, very funny book.

"GOING THAT WAY."

Captain Sinclair, of the steamer "Passport," was in a fog early one morning just before leaving Kingston and one of the passengers remarked to him that it was clear above, to which the captain answered, "Yes, but unless we have a blow-up we will not go that way."

A GOOD ONE ON CAPTAIN ESTES.

Everyone familiar with the St. Lawrence River will surely recognize the name of Estes, as it is one that has been connected with the River for the past forty years. Some one of the Utica, N. Y., daily papers mentioned Captain Estes of the steamer "St. Lawrence" as a man extremely polite and scrupulously neat in his dress, and very attentive to those who are passengers on his boat; a man who does not chew, smoke or drink, nor tell fish stories. An old gentleman, accompanied by his wife and daughter, having heard of the captain's reputation, remarked that he would like to introduce him to his daughter. The gallant captain, who looks very young for his age, answered, "No, thanks, I am a married man."

THE PHARMACEUTICAL ASSOCIATION

of the State of New York held their annual convention at the Thousand Islands two years ago, and when they made their excursion on the "Island Wanderer" around the islands I accompanied them and delineated the points of interest on the trip. Just before arriving at Central Park they noticed the large twelve-foot letters "C. P." which are used for illuminating posts at night, there being hung upon the letters one hundred lanterns. Some one asked what the "C. P." stood for. I answered, "Central Park," when one of the members, the president's wife, I think, answered "C. P." means chemically pure. I never knew it to mean anything else but that." This biographical incident is intended for druggists only.

APING CUSTOMS, MANNERS, ETC. OF THE ENGLISH.

This is done to a great extent, not only in Canada but I am sorry to say in Free America, better known as U. S. I cannot find any fault with the average Canadian, who is, as it were governed by Queen Victoria, and must have some reverence for royalty, in the aping of their manners and customs, but in this land, where we have an abundance of Queens, Princes, Lords and Sovereigns who are not flattered by titles, but bear their honors meekly, all are royal born and bred. Speaking of titles reminds me that at home I am plain Edward F. Babbage, or "Phat Boy" (I spell it with "Ph" because it does not sound so greasy), but the moment I leave home, say for a trip through the South, I am called captain for the first few hundred miles, then a little way on it becomes Colonel, and when I get to Georgia it is Major ; South Carolina it is Judge or General, until I get to Florida, and I have heard them say there, "Great God, is that you?" But we diverge. Returning to the aping of the manners of Princess Louise, I wish to say right here that I firmly believe that it did the Canadian people a great amount of good, but fail to see where the people of the United States could be benefited. I was told that at Kingston the Princess asked for her strawberries in a box with the hulls on, and when placed before her she took them up by the stem between the thumb and finger, bit the berry off and placed the hull on the plate. Now everybody does the same ; previous to her visit they used to hull and wash them before placing them on the table. The same with grapes. They used to wash them in a goblet of water at the table before eating them ; now they take the grape between the thumb and finger, press it to the lips and squeeze gently, and juice as well as insides are soon on the way to digestion, and the skin laid away on the plate as the Princess did. Asparagus—it is almost painful for me to see Canadians eat in as many ways as there were people at the table, in fact, no two ate it alike until after the Princess came ; now everybody takes it by the hard green end, between thumb and finger, and putting it into the mouth, close the teeth down upon it and draw it gently from the mouth, leaving all that is digestible within, and the remainder is laid on the plate. The Princess once took a walk through her kitchen at Rideau Hall, Ottawa, took the vegetable cook to task for washing fresh picked peas from the vine that had just been shelled, saying it was nonsense, if your hands are clean, to wash a virgin pea.

WE CALL THEM TRAMPS.

During the Centennial year many foreigners were always found among the list of passengers from every country. The proverbial English tourist cannot be mistaken by any, but this year, 1876, we had many who were too green or unsophisticated to be in that class. Now this truthful occurrence which I am about to relate is original, and occurred upon one of the Richelieu & Ontario Navigation Company's line of boats. The Englishman was relating to his newly found friend his opinion of the United States, etc., in his own peculiar style. " Hi don't like this blarsted country, you know!" "Why," said his friend, "what fault can you find with America?" " Oh, Hi've been all over it, you know, and can't find any sawciety there." " Society," said his friend, "what do you mean by society?" "Oh, dear me, you have no gentlemen or gentlemen's sons in h'America." "Why, what do you mean by gentlemen and gentlemen's sons?" "Oh, Hi mean gentlemen who never did any work, you know, nor their sons, either." "You make a mistake there, my worthy friend, we have millions of them here, but we call them tramps, and I have often thought it the best definition to a tramp I ever heard, for if there are gentlemen and their sons here who never did any work they will soon make good timber for tramps, if they are not already."

"NOT A GEORGE WASH."

He had told several very improbable stories bordering on the Eli Perkins order, and then remarked to a friend that he could not tell a lie. But the friend replied that he could the moment he heard it, and to the best of his judgment he had told several.

ROUTE OF THE STEAMER "NEW ISLAND WANDERER."

The dock from which the "New Island Wanderer" leaves for her daily excursions around the Islands, morning at 8, afternoons at 2.15, is in front of Cornwall Brothers' Stone Store, where tickets and all information may be had relative to any route by either rail or boat, to any part of the globe. Taking your position upon any part of the boat that will allow you to face the bow, upon your right will be Hart's Island, Westminster Park, Dock and Freight House, which is located at the lower end of Well's Island—this island ten miles long by four wide. A little above, hid by a cluster of trees, is the residence of John Winslow, next is Imperial Isle, owned by G. T. Rafferty, Chicago, Ill. The next is Linlithgow, owned by Hon. R. A. Livingston, New York. The next cottage on bluff is owned by Miss Lucy J. Bullock— the cottage a little above is owned by Prof. A. G. Hopkins. Next is Florence Island. Near the water edge is the boat house of St. Elmo, and the conspicuous slate-colored cottage above and wind-mill below, is owned by Mr. N. H. Hunt, of Brooklyn, N. Y. It is presumed you have taken in the above panorama before starting. Immediately after starting, on the left, you pass the Thousand Island House and Little Staples Island—around the point is Otter Creek, Edgewood Park and Martin's Cottage. The Edgewood Park Company have erected an elegant hotel and several cottages are being built by the members of the company, who form a sort of social club for their families and friends, care being exercised in the selection of members as well as visitors, and if the project is carried out, as it is contemplated, this Edgewood Park will be the summer home of some of the best people in America. On the right is Friendly Island, containing cottage, boat house and lookout, owned by E. W. Dewey, of New York. Next above is Nobby Island, owned by H. R. Heath, of New York. Opposite, on the left, is Cherry Island (the reason they call it "Cherry" is because they raise their own strawberries from which they make their celebrated custard pies). The Island contains Ingleside cottage and Melrose lodge, owned by Mr. A. B. Pullman and C. B. Marsh, of Chicago, Ill., also J. T. Easton's Villa, called Stuyvesant Cottage, and Rev. George Rockwell's cottage. Opposite on the right, is the famous Pullman Island, "Castle Rest." where George M. Pullman spent one hundred and fifty thousand dollars on buildings, etc., and presented the whole Island and surroundings to his mother on her eighty-fourth birthday. Also where Gen. U. S. Grant visited in 1872. Next beyond on bluff is "The Towers," built by W. C. Browning, of Browning, King & Co., New York. Next is Safe Point, which is on Wells' Island. On the left is the famous Devil's Rock and Oven of historic fame. It is said that here is where Bill Johnson hid himself, as there is an opening in the rock large enough for the usual fishing boat to enter with its contents and be completely hid from view. This is what is called the oven, and it resembles the old form of Dutch ovens. Beyond, on the left near the main shore, is Cuba, owned by W. F. Story of Buffalo, N. Y. Opposite, on the right, is Craig's Side, owned by H. H. Laughlin of Pittsburgh. Next, on the left, is Hill's Island and boat house, owned by C. E. Hill, of Chicago, Ill. Next, on the left, is Warner's Island. On the right is Palisade Point, owned by A. C. Beckwith. Next, on the left, is Comfort Island, owned by Mr. A. E. Clark, of the Chicago Stock Exchange. Mr. Clark has lavishly expended a large amount of money for "Comfort." It is joined to Neh-Mahben, meaning twin lakes or islands, owned by J. H. Oliphant, of New York. On the right is Louisiana Point, owned by Judge La Batte, of New Orleans, La. I desire to apologize for stating in a previous edition that Judge La Batte was dead. He came to death's door, and was so low that his physician had called his family to his bedside to witness his last moments, when he motioned to his son to come near, and drawing his ear down close to his lips, he whispered,

"Take me to my summer home on the St. Lawrence." They started from New Orleans, La., the next day and he arrived at Louisiana Point in July, and the day of this writing, August 20th, he had gained sixteen pounds in flesh and was feeling quite strong and happy—a gentleman living like the "Thane of Cawdor." Opposite, on the left, is Keppler Point, Buena Vista Lodge, owned by a gentleman from Cleveland, O., who purchased it last season. On the right is Seven Isles, owned by Gen. Bradley Winslow. McIntyre's cottage "Photo," owned by H. R. Heath, of New York, is in Dinsmore Bay, next to Seven Isles. On the left is an Indian Camp and Allegheny Point, owned by ͞ S. Laney, of Pittsburgh, Pa. A little above is Gypsy Island, owned by J. M. Curtis, of Cleveland, Ohio. Rose Island is connected with Gypsie Island by a beautiful rustic bridge. Rose Island and cottage are owned by W. G. Rose, Mayor of Cleveland, O. Opposite, on the right, is Shady Covert, a beautiful villa owned by J. C. Covert, Editor of the *Cleveland Leader*. On the right is Point Vivian, a delightful spot occupied by a stock company, mostly from Evan's Mills, N. Y. Opposite, on the right, is Island Royal, owned by Royal E. Deane, of New York. Behind Royal is Holton's Cottage, also owned by Royal E. Deane. Above, on the right, is Hill Crest, owned by General Shield's, of Philadelphia, Pa.

Nothing of interest, right or left, for the space of a mile, except Lindner's Island, until we come to Central Park (Woodbine and Crest Cottages are located here), where we make our first stop for passengers. The next island is St. Helena, owned by Harrison Stillman, of Westmoreland, N. Y. Here is a faithful representation of the tomb of Napoleon. Brown's Bay on the right and Swan's Bay on the left. A little above on the left is Little Calumet, owned by J. D. Green, of Boston, Mass. Above, on the main shore, is the cottage of J. B. Collins. Opposite, on the right, may be seen the celebrated Limburger Cheese Factory. Opposite, on the main shore, left, is the farm and house of Captain Jack, the mill and dock somewhat dilapidated. Opposite is Island Blanche and cottage, E. E. Buckingham, owner. A little opposite is Paul's dock and Sunny Side, with three other villas; also a dairy farm, which, from its fine looking barns, sheds and house must be considered very prosperous. Peel's Dock having been rebuilt, was memorable as the spot where the vessel "Sir Robert Peel" as burned in retaliation for the "Caroline" being sent over Niagara Falls. Next on the right, "Jolly Oaks," Twin Cottage Home, Pleasant View and San Souci's, four cottages and dock. The pretty little summer house on the Island passed, we arrive at Fern Cliff cottages and dock. A large stone cottage was erected here several seasons ago, called Hiawatha Cottage. This is for sale. Beautiful villas, camps and cottages line the banks on the right, among which is Fair View, owned by Hon. W. W. Butterfield, of Redwood, N. Y., until we arrive at Fair View. Opposite, on the left, is Fisher's Landing, Robinson Island, Johnson's Light and Cottage, Hemlock, Cedar, and other islands, around the point is Castle Chase, and we come in sight of Thousand Island Park—located at the upper end of Wells' Island, owned and controlled by the Methodists; the neatest and most orderly and attractive resort among the Islands. Something should be said here regarding this, the most celebrated spot among the Thousand Islands. As it is impossible, from my limited knowledge, to do the subject justice, and, as I cannot steal, clip, borrow or plagiarize from any other work, I can only say, stay over one day, or until the boat comes back, and look over this delightful spot.

Again on our way, we pass the head of Wells' Island, and have a view on the right of the finest avenue in the Park, a long line of boat houses, and a number of steam yachts, sail and fishing boats, windmills, etc., etc. Beyond, on the right in the distance, is Hemlock Island and Hotel, owned by Mr. Garrison, of Syracuse. This Island, now called Murray Hill Park, was purchased by the Thousand Island Improvement Co., and if the energy displayed continues this spot will in a short time become the beauty of the whole. The large body of water on the right is Eel Bay. On the right is Grennel's Island and House, where the boat stops for passengers; beyond, on the right, is Otsego Point and Cottages. We next pass two cottages, after which Picton Isle. Next is the Berg group; beyond are the Packingham Islands; in the distance on the left is Round Island Park and the "Frontenac" Hotel; many magnificent cottages line the shores all around the Island. This is a favorite resort of the Baptists. On the right is Little Round Island, and on the left in the Bay is Washington Island; opposite on the right is the celebrated Calumet Island, owned by Chas. G. Emery of Old Judge cigarette fame. In the distance, front, is Clayton. The depot and docks of the R. W. & O. R. R. are located here. Opposite is Gov. Alvord's Island. After leaving Clayton, on the left you will have a view of Prospect Park and Hill, a delightful resort. Next on the left, as we turn, is Blanket Island; on the right is Grindstone and Club Island; next on the right is Hen Island, owned by W. F. Morgan; Whisky Island is owned by C. Wolfe, of New York, also Levett's Island, owned by H. G. Levett; near by is Buck's Point, owned by Ives Crocker, and Rum Point, owned by Hervy and Hewett Morgan, of Washington, D. C.; Hicks, near Amblers is owned by relatives in the Bay at Buck's Point, is the finest bathing beach among the Islands ; beyond is the celebrated Wolf or Long Island, the largest of the Thousand Islands, being twenty-one miles long ; next is Hickory Island. We now cross the dividing line, after which many islands appear, all sizes and shapes until we come to Ross Dick Island ; beyond is Burnt Island ; light in the distance is Red Horse Light ; opposite on the right, is Kalaria, owned by Prof. Castle, of Toronto, Canada, and occupied by Wilmot Castle and his brother Arthur, and families, this season ; Wilmot Castle & Co., of Rochester, N. Y.,—the manufacturers of the Arnold automatic cooker. We have used one in our family for the past five years, and I think more of it than I do of " my mother-in-law," and she was one of the best women that ever lived.

AMONG THE ISLANDS.

It must not be supposed that these hundreds of islands are all occupied and have cottages on them, or laid out with walks or fountains. For every island that has a house on it there are perhaps twenty that have not. The number of houses are increasing every year, and I think that in time nearly every island will be occupied in the Canadian Channel as they are in the American. We next arrive at

GANANOQUE.

Here the captain announces a stay of twenty-five minutes for refreshments, remarking, also, that it takes twelve minutes to walk up town and twelve minutes back, with the remainder to refresh, which seems to my mind a little too fresh. Leaving Gananoque on time, we will return by the Canadian Channel, which is more wild and picturesque, as far as scenery is concerned, although not one island or point is inhabited here to ten in the American Channel. On the right is Kipp Island. Passing many beautiful islands and light houses, we arrive at Halstead's Bay—after passing which the islands come thick and fast, all sizes and shapes, from a little one for a cent to those done up in bunches, like asparagus, and you get a bunch for five. We pass very close to Ash Island, so near that moss has been plucked by passengers on the boat. We soon arrive at Lind Light, on the right, and are coming to the, Fiddler's Elbow. Lay this book aside at this point and feast the eye, for no writer could do the subject of a description justice. The King of Dwarfs, Gen. Tom Thumb, was a passenger on the "Wanderer" one day when he asked the captain why he could not have an island. The captain with his usual generosity, gave him one just his size, and to commemorate the event has placed a monument there to his memory. We soon emerge from our land, or island-locked channel, and approach Darling's Dock. The dock is visible, but we have never seen the darling —after which comes Echo point, where you can hear as many echos as you pay cents fare. Passing a farm-house on the right, we soon arrive on the left at Rockport; here you will observe we have but two seasons of the year, Ice and Rock; this is the Rocky season.

Turning to the right, we make direct for Westminster Park. Looking backward over the left shoulder, you will have a view of Idlewilde and Sport Islands, formerly owned by the Packers, of Pennsylvania, who expended seventy-eight thousand dollars to beautify this spot, now owned by E. P. Wilber, Pres. of the Lehigh Valley R. R. & Coal Co. A better view of those islands may be obtained after leaving Westminster Park for Alexandria Bay. After passing the point, Hayden's Island, Fairyland comes in view. The little island with cottage, is owned by Mr. Hasbrouck, of Ogdensburg, N. Y., called Pike Island. The next on the right is St. John's Island, owned by Judge Donahue, of New York. The next on the right is Manhatten group, owned by Judge Spencer and Hasbrouck, of New York. A wooden bridge joins them together. This is the first island inhabited for recreation, and was bought by Seth Green, the fish culturist of New York State ; on the left is long Beach, and Anthony's Point, (the Ledges owned by C. J. Hudson, of New York) and Bonnie Castle ; on the right is Deshler and Hart's Island. We next arrived at Alexandria Bay, from which we started almost four hours ago.

"YES! A GREAS-Y STATUE."

"How much do you weigh?" Well, I am asked that question many times every day, and as I am not sensitive will say my weight is three hundred and thirty-three pounds in the shade, just one pound for every mile between Toronto and Montreal via Grand Trunk Railway. The reason why I say in the shade, is because there has never been raised a mathematician with the ability to compute the weight of a grease spot, and were

I compelled to remain in the sun very long would make one, and do not care to mislead people into an error. The fat of this land is about as unevenly distributed as the wealth. Those who ain't got it want it; those who have it, have too much. I am, therefore, a Vanderbilt in grease, have a corner in lard, as it were.

"DO YOU GO OUT FISHING?"

Well, not often. You see, this ponderous body of mine does not fit the average fishing boat. My fears are not all bound up in that one fact, nor in the satisfaction that if the boat should upset that I would not sink, but the fear that is indelibly photographed upon my mind, that as I would float, and being so large, some steamboat captain or pilot would take me for an island, lay alongside and let the passengers off for a little picnic or an hour's pleasure. Think of it.

YACHTING.

Water—and as one enthusiastic writer puts it—such water!—is abundant, and to enjoy this water in a pensive or poetic mood, the steam yacht should be brought into requisition. Private yachts are numerous and elegant, and it is to the credit of the owners that they are not niggardly in exhibiting a spirit of generosity and courtesy. They are constantly inviting individuals and parties to enjoy the exhilarating excitement of the shooting around the beautiful spots. And if you, dear tourist, have no friend that invites you to share a cushioned seat in his graceful fairy-like craft, then go to Capt. Reese, on the "New Island Wanderer," who will take you on an excursion among the islands that you will gladly recall as a cheerful reminiscence of your St.

Lawrence excursion, for the opportunity will have been offered to bring within the range of your vision enchanting scenes that pen is not adequate to describe, but by purchasing one of the " Phat Boy's " Pictures of the St. Lawrence, you will be the possessor of the only correct map, a perfect guide to the river.

"WOULD YOU BELIEVE IT?"

A gentleman from London came on board the boat at Kingston one morning, rushed up to me and said, " Mr. Babbage, how do you do? Why, you cannot imagine haw glad I am to see you! Why, do you know that before I left 'home' a lady invited me to take tea at her house, and when I told her that I was coming to America she never stopped ta'king about you for over two hours; it is a great relief to meet you, I assure you." Meeting upon the street one afternoon, a very fine looking old gentleman, he said, "Hold on a moment, I have something to tell you. I have just received a letter from my daughter who lives in Australia, she said she found one of your books upon the table at her friend's house where she was visiting so she inquired how it came there. "Why, bless your soul, we took a trip with him down the St. Lawrence River and he made it pleasant for us for eight hours and I would not part with the book for an interest in the profits of the 'new version' or revised edition."

A lady wrote me from Trenton, N. J. "While at Alexandria Bay in 1883, I bought a copy of the 'Phat Boy's Delineations of the St. Lawrence River (I think of the author from the picture on the cover). Have read it over and over to my friends until it is completely worn out. Can you forward me another copy?" I did as requested and at the same time inquired what pleased her friends most. And she said in reply, that it was all good, but the articles upon myself were the most pleasing to her. I must, therefore, send her a copy of this, my last effort. The latter part of May I met a gentleman at the Sturtevant House, New York, while visiting Mr. J. C. Matthews, the proprietor, who said : " How do you do, Mr. Babbage ? I presume you do not remember me, but while at the Thousand Islands last season, and before going to Montreal, I purchased of you one of your books, and it would be an injustice not to tell you that we had more real pleasure and profit from its perusal than any one thing on our trip. I desire to thank you, and my wife would do the same were she here. The book is almost worn out ; more than fifty of my friends have read it. I want another copy ; if you will not send it, I will come to Alexandria Bay and get it."

H. H. WARNER AND GEO. M. PULLMAN.

Two of nature's noble men. Two of the greatest benefactors of the human race. Two of the greatest men born in New York State. One the inventor of the clebrated Pullman car that has given ease, rest and comfort to the whole enlightened world. The other, the Warner's Safe Cure, which has given relief to millions of sufferers from kidney and liver disease.

Each in turn are spending a small portion of their immense wealth in building suitable cottages upon their respective islands, "Warner's" and "Pullman's which they expect to occupy during the coming season. When such men as they are, do what they intend, it will prove to the world that the Thousand Islands, as a watering place, has no equal, and by next season we may look for a "boom" beyond our greatest expectation.

THE "LOTUS SEEKER."

This tidy little craft made its first appearance on the St. Lawrence three seasons ago and is owned by Mr. Holden, of New York, who has a very beautiful cottage at Thousand Island Park. Many times during the season she could be seen plying in and out among the islands, comfortably filled with the invited guests of her owner, and passing every thing moved by steam power. I felt quite badly one day while taking a ride upon one of the "cracked" yachts, to be passed so quickly by the "Lotus Seeker" that I did not have time to say good-bye to my friend, J. W. Burdick, Gen. Passenger Agent of the D. & H. R. R. Co., who was one of her passengers.

WALTER H. GRIFFIN,

the present room clerk at the Thousand Island House, (late of Hotel Marlborough, New York), was the winner of the prize for the largest pickerel catch of 1884. It was caught within one hundred yards of the hotel and weighed eighteen and three-quarter pounds.

MR. J. C. MATTHEWS,

who was the manager of the Thousand Island House in 1884, is inquired after by visitors more than any other person. I hope to be saved some trouble, as well as time, by stating here that he is the proprietor of the Sturtevant House, New York. If you visit the city give him a call.

LORD DUFFERIN,

one of Canada's former Governor-Generals, and in my opinion the best they ever had, was a passenger down the St. Lawrence many times while I was guide to the river. How well I remember some one asking him why he left Toronto and his comfortable quarters at the Queen's Hotel to come to Montreal. He answered by stating, that over across the lake in the United States, they had just had an election, the Tilden and Hayes campaign, and as it was impossible to tell who was really chosen by the people, he was afraid they, the people, would rise in their might, send a deputation over to Toronto, kidnap him and place him in the presidential chair. Then what would become of poor little Canada.

"A LITTLE ONE ON PERKINS."

Two gentlemen at the Marsden House one day were talking, when the subject of truth was approached, and one of them who stammered, said, " There are t-t-three great li-liars i-i-in America." The friend said, " Who are they?" "O-o-one of t-t-them i-i-is T-T-Tom Oc-Oc-Ochiltree of Te-Te-Texas, and th-th-the other two is E-E-Eli Perkins."

VISITORS AT THE THOUSAND ISLANDS

who desire to see Montreal and return by boat (their time being limited), the following information will be of interest. All passengers arrive in Montreal between six and seven o'clock P. M., as there is little to see at night and very little time to see it in. The boat leaves her dock, Canal Basin, to return, every morning at 9 o'clock except Sunday. You can remain in Montreal until the 12 M. train for Lachine from the G. T. R. station (by taking the train, fare 25 cents, you will arrive at Lachine in time to take the boat and enjoy your dinner while passing through Lake St. Louis). Should you desire to prolong your stay, remain in Montreal until the 5 P. M. train leaves same depot for Coteau Landing. A carriage in waiting will take you to the boat, fare from Montreal, including carriage, $1.25. You will take passage from there at seven o'clock, and have your supper on board the boat while passing through Lake St. Francis. It takes the boat sixteen hours longer to come back than to go down (reason they are compelled to pass through the Lachine, Beauharnois and Cornwall canals, which consumes the time). All passengers arrive at Alexandria Bay, every day, between twelve and one o'clock P. M., except on Monday.

WHAT I KNOW ABOUT CATCHING FISH

During last summer I was at Alexandria Bay, N. Y., and took note of some of the best catches of fish, but I have not the space to record them. Let me say that anybody can catch fish of the following varieties anywhere in the St. Lawrence River : Rock bass, black bass, perch, pike, pickerel and muscalonge. I have caught, off the dock at the Bay, in less than two hours, a black bass weighing three and one-half pounds and a pickerel weighing over six pounds. The largest fish caught last season was a muscalonge, weight 38 lbs., caught at an Island opposite the bay near Rockport. A pike 7½ pounds, black bass 5½ pounds, a pickerel 13 pounds. Several fishing parties out for one to three days brought in such enormous catches that if I mentioned them they would be called fish stories.

Respectfully yours,
E. F. BABBAGE.

A REAL LIVE DUDE

was at the Bay last season, and I must give him credit for one thing, I could not for having either money or brains, but will say he was very attentive to the ladies, and it may be said to his credit, he never tried to cut me out. One fine morning he induced three of the nicest young ladies at the Bay to take a boat ride, and for the privilege of their company agreed to do the rowing himself. They had been out upon the water for some time, and he had done the rowing heroically, but getting into the strong current, his physical development was being tested to the utmost, when he asked the young ladies "if it would not be better for him to hug the shore." After a pause of a minute, the girliest girl of the group exclaimed: "Well, if you can't find anything better to hug, do for heaven's sake 'hug the shore!'"

E. B. WARREN, OF PHILADELPHIA, PA.,

with his wife and daughters, have in the past paid the St. Lawrence River many visits, and been mentioned by me for their fish catches. One day in particular they brought in and exhibited at the Thousand Island House, 18 small mouthed black bass weghing seventy-four pounds. Since the completion of "The Sagamore" on Green Island, Lake George, and the build-

ing of an elegant cottage there, he stays at home, and
I am contented with the old proverb, "Tho' lost to
sight to memory dear."

EDWARD INGRAHAM,

the King of Connecticut Clock Manufactures, whose
immense factories are located at Bristol, Conn., was
spending a few days at "The Sagamore," Lake George,
in order to gain strength after recovery from a severe
attack of pneumonia. The bracing air of this locality, together with two hours spent in a social chat
with a select circle of the guests (myself included), he
said it would be sure to produce the desired effect—
health and strength. I mean to time him with an
eight day clock and see. I have timed him. And
hope his health exceeds his generosity, which I know
is very large, because we are indebted to him for the
ticking of the prettiest clock that graces any mantle
on our street.

E. G. GILMORE,

New York's greatest Theatrical Manager, has enjoyed
many seasons of pleasure at Alexandria Bay. The last
time I saw him, he wanted to know how it would do
for him to bring his whole corps de ballet to the
Thousand Islands for a season's recuperation. "Don't
you think it would give them vigor, such good bracing air as you have up there?"

MESSRS. RAYMOND AND WHITCOMB,

America's greatest Excursion agents, have probably
brought more people to the St. Lawrence River, than

have come directly from the reading of the several editions of my book that have been issued during the past nine years, which is saying a great deal for them. I hope to have the pleasure of meeting more of their select parties during the coming season.

MR. AND MRS. CHAS. MAC EVOY,

of New York, have been visitors at the Thousand Islands many times. Mr. MacEvoy has persevered and after many years succeeded in producing "Glazed Kid," the most superb of shoe materials, "out-vieing France." My Auntie May, who weighs two hundred and sixty-five pounds, after wearing a pair of shoes four months made of this material, says, "the wearing qualities of the glazed kid produced the best results of any she ever wore." One season, with a New York friend, they caught the largest catch of black bass I ever saw brought in by amateurs.

DR. PERRY OF THE UNITED STATES HOTEL,

Saratoga Springs, caught the largest muscalonge of the season 1886. As the fishing is much better every year, on account of all illegal fishing with nets having been stopped, I hope to see him again at the Bay, as well as all other lovers of fishing.

THE NAMES OF THE INHABITED ISLANDS, POINTS AND COTTAGES

In the American Channel of the River; Alphabetically arranged.

A
Alleghney Point	J. S. Laney.
Arcadia and Ina	S. A. Driggs.
Alice	Col. A. J. Casse.
Ambler	Mrs. Steul.

B
Bergshire	Hon. S. G. Pope.
Bay Side	H. B. Mosher.
Bonny Eyrie	Mrs. Peck.
Bay View	C. S. Lyman.
Bo.'e Island	Rev. Walter Ayrat
Bolla Vista Lodge	R. B. Chisholm.
Bonny Castle (Main Land)	Mrs. J. G. Hollar 1.
Birch Island	W. J. Lewis.
Buck's Point	Ives Crocker.

C
Castle Fannie	Rev. W. Dempster nase.
Covert	J. C. Overt.
Cloud Rest	A. H. Green
Chillon	A. H. Greenw
Calum	Chas. G. Emory.
Cedar Island	J. M. Curtis.
Comfort Island	A. E. Clark.
Craig Side (Well's Island)	H. A. Laughlin.
Crescent Cottages (Main Land)	Bleecker Van Wagenen.

D
Devil's Oven	H. R. Heath.
Deshler Island	W. G. Deshler.
Deer Island	Hon. S. Miller.
Douglass Island	Douglass Miller.
Dinglespell	Joseph Babcock.

E
Elephant Rock	T. C. Crittenden.
Easton, Stuyvesant, Cherry Island	James E. Easton.
Edgewood Park	Edgewood Park Association.
Edgewood Cottage	G. C. Martin.
Elm Island	R. E. Hungerford.
Excelsior Group	C. S. Goodwin.
Elinore	Wm. McAfee.

F
Frederick Island	C. L. Fredericks.
Fisher's Landing	Mrs. R. Gurnee & Miss Newton.
Friendly	E. W. Dewey.
Florence Island	H. S. Chandler.
Felsencck	Prof. A. G. Hopkins.
Fern	N. & J. Wilson.
Fairy Land	C. H. & W. B. Hayden.

G
Governor's Island	Hon. T. G. Alvord.
Gun Island	H. H. Warner.
Goose Island	Mrs. Lottie Simonds.
Gypsy Island	J. M. Curtis.

H

Helen's Island ... Mrs. O. G. Staples.
Hemlock ... Hon. W. F. Porter and Wilson.
Hub Island ... George W. Bost.
Holloway's Point ... Nathan Holloway.
Harmony ... Mrs. C. Berger.
Hub Clark Island ... Will Clark.
Hart's Island ... Hon. E. K. Hart.
Huguenot ... L. Hasbrouck.
Hen Island ... W. F. Morgan.
Hicks Island ... J. Q. Holland.

I

Isle Helen ... Mrs. Helen S. Taylor.
Isle of Pines ... Mrs. E. N. Robinson.
Island Royal ... Royal E. Deane.
Island Gracie ... Miss G. Fox.
Ingleside (Cherry Island) ... G. B. Marsh.
Imperial Island ... G. T. Rafferty.
Island Mary ... W. M. Palmer.
Idlewild ... Mrs. R. A. Packer.
Island Blanch ... Watertown, N. Y.

J

Jefferson Island ... E. P. Gardiner.
Jolly Oaks (Wells' Island) ... Prof. A. H. Brown and others.

K

Killien's Point ... Mr. J. Killien.
Kit Grafton ... Mrs. S. L. George.

L

Little Calumet ... Oliver H. Green.
Lone Pine ... Comstock & Co.
Little Charm Island ... Mrs. F. W. Baker.
Look Out Island ... Thos. H. Borden.
Little Lehigh ... C. H. Cummings.
Little Fraud ... R. Pease.
Long Branch ... Mrs. C. E. Clark.
Little Delight ... L. W. Morrison.
Long Rock ... W. F. Wilson.
Little Whortleberry ... Mrs. L. E. B. Brown.
Lattimer ... Dr. C. E. Lattimer.
Lindner's ... John Lindner.
Louisiana Point ... Judge La Bette.
Little Gem ... Mrs. V. Walton.
Little Angel ... W. A. Angell.
Linlithgow ... Hon. R. A. Livingston.
Lily's Island ... L. R. H. Morrison.
Levetts ... H. G. Levetts.

M

Maple Island ... Joseph Atwell.
Minium ... Rev. W. W. Walsh.
Melrose Lodge (Cherry Island) ... A. B. Pullman.
Manhattan ... J. L. Hasbrouck, J.C. Spencer.
Maple Island ... J. L. Hasbrouck.

N

Nemah-bin ... J. H. Oliphant.
Nobby Island ... H. R. Heath.
Nett's Island ... W. B. Hayden.

O

One Tree Island ... William Wright.
Occident and Orient ... E. W. Washburn.
Ours Island ... Mrs. M. Carter.

P

Peel Island.................................Mrs. S. P. Lake and others.
Point Vivian...............................R. T. Evans and others.
Photo Island...............................H. R. Hoath.
Pullman Island............................George M. Pullman.
Point Lookout (Well's Island).........Miss. L. J. Bullock.
Picnic Point................................Westminster Park Ass'n.
Point Marguerite (Main Island)......E. Anthony.
Pike Island................................Frank F. Dickinson.
Palisade Point............................A. C. Beckwith.

Q

Quartette Island..........................Mrs. W. Egan.

R

Rob Roy Island...........................A. H. Greenwalt.
River Side Island........................James C. Leo.
Resort Island.............................W. J. Lewis.
Round Island.............................Baptist Association.
Rum Point.................................H. & H. Morgan, Wash & Co.

S

Schooner Island..........................J. N. Whitehouse.
Sunbeam Group........................Odd Fellows of Watertown.
Spuyten Duyvel..........................Alice P. Sargent.
Summer-Land............................Summer-Land Association.
Sunny-Side Island......................W. Stevenson.
Seven Isles...............................Hon. Bradley Winslow.
Sunny Side (Cherry Islands).......Rev. George Rockwell.
Safe Point (Well's Island)............H. H. Warner.
St. Elmo...................................N. H. Hunt.
Sun-Dew Island.........................Chas. M. Slamm.
St. John's.................................Judge Donohue.
Sport Island..............................H. C. Wilber.
St. Helena................................Harrison Stillman.

T

Two Islands, Eel Bay..................Dr. E. L. Sargent.
Twin Islands..............................I. L. Huntington.
Throop Dock..............................Dr. O. E. Lattimer and others.
The Ledges...............................Mrs. J. L. Hudson.
Thousand Island Park.................Methodist Association.
The Towers................................W.C.Browning, New York.

U

Una Island................................Mrs. M. E. Steel.

V

Vanderbilt Island........................J. B. Hamilton.
Vilula Island..............................H. Sisson.

W

Walton Island............................J. N. & G. H. Robinson.
West View Island........................Hon. S. G. Pope.
Welcome Island..........................Hon. S. G. Pope.
Whortleberry Island....................Mrs. Etta Stillwell.
Watch Island.............................Mrs. Elizabeth Skinner.
Waving Branches.......................H. S. Ainsworth.
Wild Rose..................................Hon. W. G. Rose.
Warner Island............................H. H. Warner.
Wau Winet................................C. E. Hill.
West Point.................................John Mathews.
Whiskey....................................C. Wolfe, N. Y.

Route A.

N. Y. C. & H. R. R. R.

The New York Central & Hudson River Railroad, aptly termed "America's Greatest Railroad," reaches more celebrated health and pleasure resorts than probably any other line in the United States, and has long been the favorite route with tourists to Saratoga, Lake George, Lake Champlain and the Catskill Mountains, Montreal, Adirondack Mountains, Thousand Islands, Richfield and Sharon Springs, Cooperstown, Niagara Falls, and hundreds of other noted resorts of New York State, New England and Canada.

The New York Central is the only four-track railroad in the world, and enjoys the unique distinction of being the only trunk line with a passenger station in the City of New York, all trains arriving at and departing from Grand Central Station, Fourth Avenue and Forty-Second Street, the very centre of the city.

With its magnificent roadway, easy curves, light grades, superb equipment and historic scenery, the New York Central presents the highest developments of the modern art of transport.

Route B.

WEST SHORE ROUTE,

N. Y. C. & H. R. R. R., LESSEES.

THE TOURISTS' ROUTE TO THE NORTH.

While many suppose that both sides of the Hudson River present equal attractions—and it would be hard to decide which is the most beautiful—it is a curious fact that all, or nearly all, the noted summer resorts for which the country adjacent is famous, are located on its western bank. Thus, starting from New York and following up the West Shore Route, we find the Palisades, Tappan, Rockland Lake, Stony Point, Cranston's, West Point, Cornwall, Lake Mohonk and Minnewaska, the Catskills, Saratoga, Mount McGregor, and the Adirondacks.

In addition to the above points of interest, the traveler may be conveyed to Lake George, Lake Champlain and Montreal on the north; Sharon Springs, Cooperstown, Richfield Springs, Thousand Islands and the Lake Region of Central New York, or take the New York Central Railroad from the Grand Central station and proceed on the world-renowned four track road to Utica, where direct connection can be made with the Utica and Black River branch of the Rome, Watertown and Ogdensburg Railroad—N. Y. C. & H. R. R. R., Lessees—which in a few hours will bring you to the majestic scenery of the St. Lawrence. At Clayton you take one of the beautiful steamers of the Richelieu and Ontario Navigation Company, direct for Montreal, or continue on by rail to Rochester. Should you remain over, stop at the New Osburn House, kept by my friend, Elmer E. Almy, or continue to

BUFFALO, N. Y.

which is connected with Toronto by the Grand Trunk R. R., the new route, leaving Erie Depot at 8:15 A. M. by rail to Port Dalhousie connecting with the steamer for Toronto, arriving at 12:55 P. M., connecting with Royal Mail Line for Thousand Islands and Montreal,—should you conclude to remain over at Buffalo for a day or more stop at the Hotel Niagara, kept by as genial a landlord as one wishes to meet, Mr. H. A. Dunn,—or proceed by rail to

NIAGARA FALLS.

When visiting this wonder of wonders at any season of the year, the tourist will find a number of hotels to choose from. The Spencer House recommended in this book as being a first class house and open the year around burned down last March.

GRAND TRUNK R. R.

Trains leave Niagara Falls every morning, Sundays excepted, by Grand Trunk R. R. direct for Toronto, arriving in time to connect with the Mail Line for Montreal. Trains leave Niagara Falls every morning, except Sunday, at 9:45 A. M. via Central Hudson branch for Lewiston. Any information relative to the route or the purchase of tickets will be cheerfully given upon application to Mrs. L. Barber, who can be found at room No. 1, of the International Hotel Building.

At Lewiston connections are made with the fast sailing side-wheel steamboats

"CHICORA" AND "CIBOLA,"

making three trips daily across the beautiful Lake Ontario, arriving at Toronto in time to connect with the Richelieu and Ontario Navigation Company for Kingston, Alexandria Bay, Thousand Islands and Rapids of the St. Lawrence to Montreal.

TORONTO,

the capital of the Province of Ontario, is situated on a circular bay of the same name, and was founded by Governor Simcoe in 1794, and we advise all tourists to make a stay of one or two days here. It is the only Americanized city in the Dominion of Canada. The Queens Royal Hotel, situated at Niagara on the Niagara river, and the Queen's Hotel, at Toronto, are presided over by Messrs. McGaw and Winnett. This is one of the largest and most comfortable hotels in the Dominion of Canada, and, being adjacent to the

Lake, commands a splendid view of Toronto Bay and Lake Ontario. It is well known as one of the coolest houses in summer in Canada, and is elegantly furnished throughout. Rooms *en suite*, with bath-rooms attached, on every floor. The Queens has been liberally patronized by Royalty and Nobility during their visits to Toronto, and among those who have honored it with their patronage, are His Imperial Highness, the Grand Duke Alexis, of Russia ; their Royal Highnesses, Prince Leopold, Prince George, Princess Louise, and the Duke and Duchess of Connaught, the Marquis of Lorne, the Earl and Countess of Dufferin, the Marquis and Marchioness of Lansdowne, Lord and Lady Stanley of Preston, and the best families. If you desire a carriage while in the city, Telephone to No. 109, R. Bond's livery, York Street. His new establishment is the largest and most commodious in the Dominion of Canada and contains every style of equipage run on wheels, from the Dog Cart to the Tally-Ho Coach—everything first-class in that line.

PORT HOPE

is situated 65 miles from Toronto. A small stream which here falls into the lake, has formed a valley in which the town is located. The harbor at the mouth of the stream is shallow, but safe and commodious. Port Hope is a pretty town ; on the western side the hills rise gradually one above the other. The highest summit, called " Fort Orton," affords a fine prospect, and overlooks the country for a great distance. The village is incorporated ; population about 5,114. A direct route to Rochester by the steamer " Norseman " leaves this port every morning, except Sunday, calling at Cobourg and connecting with Grand Trunk train from Toronto every week day morning and arriving in Rochester the same afternoon. The Grand Summer Excursion of the "Norseman" from Rochester to Alexandria Bay leaves Rochester every Saturday afternoon and passing though the 1,000 Island scenery of the St. Lawrence River, arrives at Alexandria Bay in time for dinner, giving the passengers about five hours at the Bay, and returns to Rochester early on Monday. I have advised many of my friends to make this trip, all of whom have expressed themselves as delighted.

Also from this port the R. I. S. & O., Nav. Co. Str., makes three trips a week leaving Charlotte Tuesdays Thursdays and Saturdays at 5:30 P. M., and returning on Mondays Wednesdays and Fridays giving the passengers a delightful trip

COBOURG,

seven miles below Port Hope, contains 6,000 inhabitants. It has seven churches, two banks, three grist mills, two foundries, and the largest cloth factory in the Province. It is also the seat of Victoria College, and Theological Institute. Midway between Port Hope and Cobourg is "Duck Island," on which a lighthouse is maintained by the government.

FROM KINGSTON TO MONTREAL.

The Mail Line, or Richelieu Co.'s boats, leave Kingston every morning at five o'clock. As we proceed down the river, a description of the city will be in order.

Kingston has a population of 15,000, was founded in 1672, by Governor De Courcelles, receiving the name of Fort Cataraqui. Later, a massive stone fort was built by Count De Frontenac, and received his name. In 1762 the place was taken by the British, who gave it its present name. As a place of defense it stands next in strength to Quebec. The batteries of Fort Henry are calculated for the reception of numerous cannon and mortars of the largest calibre. These together with neighboring martello towers, form a formidable defense against any aggressive movement which might be directed against the city. These fortifications are seen to excellent advantage from the steamer soon after it leaves the dock.

On the right is Garden Island ; on the left, Cedar Island, and behind is Fort Henry. There is here, also in view, the round stone towers referred to above. Near the middle of the river is Wolf or Long Island, 21 miles long, and 7 miles wide near the western end. There is nothing either of romance or historical episode to weave into our story concerning the inhabitants of this, the largest of the Thousand Island group. Suffice it to say, that the territory is a portion of the Dominion of Canada, and that the habits of civilized life characterize the people. A Canal is cut through Wolf Island and the Steamer Maud runs through, forming a ferry to Cape Vincent, N. Y. Between one channel and the main land there is St. John's or Howe Island, of no mean proportions.

Ordinarily, we have now spent about one hour on the steamer from Kingston, and come to the point in the channel where we must diverge either for Gananoque or Clayton. We are bound for Clayton and the American channel of the St. Lawrence River. (For description of Gananoque and the Canadian channel, see Route of the " Island Wanderer, " page 49.)

The time is early morning, the sun quite bright, and the atmosphere remarkably clear. The scene is now attractive. Look ahead in the distance a little to the left, and you will behold the eagle tree. Hundreds have been deceived with the idea that it was an actual live eagle, spreading its wings and soaring aloft to a height that the imagination can scarcely reach. It is a delusion ; 'tis nothing but a tree, as its true features, or rather beautiful foliage, has deceived the eye of the novice of this region.

On the left is Grindstone Island. On it is an organized community. The inhabitants are farmers, and for the education of whose children a school is maintained. The Island Grindstone derived its name from a vessel loaded with grindstones striking the Island under full sail, the vessel sank but the grindstones floated. Telling this story one day to a crowd of passengers, one of the ladies, Mrs. E. P. Hannaford, wife of the chief engineer of the Grand Trunk R. R., added that she knew the circumstances and that the Anchor swam ashore. This caused me to smile, when she added, "That was the captain's name." On the right is Clayton.

It may be well to state here that authorities (?) differ as to how many islands there really are. Som say fifteen hundred ; some eighteen hundred, and others carefully write, *nearly* two thousand. Life is too short for us to stop and count these natural beauties, and even the pilots have no desire to win fame as statisticians by asserting the correct number. The "Phat Boy" has just issued the only correct map of the St. Lawrence River published, which will not be misleading to the student of the minute details. But we digress.

CAPE VINCENT

is a pleasant little village in Jefferson county, N. Y., at the junction of Lake Ontario and the St. Lawrence River. It is also the terminus of the Rome, Watertown & Ogdensburg Railroad, and connections are made here with the Thousand Island Steamboat Company's line of steamboats. This company owns most of the steamboats which ply through, around, across or otherwise in the Thousand Islands. Among the fleet may be found the palace steamers " St. Lawrence, " " Islander," "Maynard," " Jessie Bain, " "Maud, " etc., etc., one of which will convey passengers arriving by R., W. & O. R. R. to Alexandria Bay. Connections are made to Kingston by steamer " Maud. "

A canal having been constructed through Wolf Island the steamer " Maud "passes through thus saving a trip above the head of Wolf Island or about the same distance passing around the foot to reach Kingston, since the N. Y. C. & H. R. R. became lessees of the R., W. & O. a bridge is contemplated to cross the river at Cape Vincent, to connect it with Kingston, Canada.

Let us here describe the American channel from Cape Vincent.

As we steam out of this port, on the left is Long or Wolf Island. The next on the right is

CARLTON ISLAND.

At the upper extremity the land narrows into a rugged promontory, ending in a bluff sixty feet in height. Here,. lifting their ruined heads aloft, and plainly visible to all passers along the river, stand a number of toppling and half ruined chimneys. These may be seen for miles around. So long have these old sentinels watched over the scenes that their history is lost in the misty past. Around them are the remaining ruins of an old fort, supposed by many to be the ruins of old Fort Frontenac. In its old redoubts and parapets linger antiquated historical legends and traditions enough to fill a volume, which has been lately published by the editor of the *St. Lawrence News*, of Clayton, N. Y., forming an interesting study. A copy was presented to me by the publisher, but has been mislaid and cannot be found. An ancient well, cut in the solid Trenton limestone down to the level of the lake, has been converted by the reckless imaginations of the natives into a receptacle of the golden doubloons which the French soldiers, upon evacuating the old fort, are said to have thrown there, with the brass guns on top of them. Upon either side and immediately in front of the bluff upon which the old fort stands, is a quiet, pretty little bay, which may once have supplied a safe and easy anchorage for the vessels that lay under its protecting guns.

The fortress is supposed to have been one of importance as a military post at some time, having been built upon an excellent plan and in the most substantial manner. Numbers of graves still occupy a field near by, the remains of the brave soldiers who once occupied the fort. The scene is of deep interest to the student of history. This island has been purchased by the Folger Brothers, and laid out in villa lots. A *grand barbecue* and sale was held here in 1889 and many lots were purchased by wealthy parties who intend to build upon the Island the coming season, and I have no doubt this will be one of the most popular resorts of the Thousand Islands. It is also used for picnics and pleasure parties.

About six miles this side of Clayton is Lindsay Island, the only one on the right between Cape Vincent and Clayton, except Carlton Island just spoken of.

CLAYTON

is in the American channel. In the distant front, just before landing, we have a magnificent view of Prospect Park and hill, a delightful spot for recreation and pleasure. No better view can be had of the islands and surrounding country than from the eminence of the hill. Clayton is our first stopping place. It is a village that derives its importance to tourists as being the terminus of the R., W. & O. R. R., Utica and Black River Division, and here it is where passengers from the East generally get their first glimpse of the St. Lawrence. There are three good hotels, the Hubbard, Walton and the Windsor; kept by as genial landlords as ever lived, and from the town many fishing parties go out daily. The Thousand Island Company steamers run from this point in connection with the above named railroads to Alexandria Bay and other landing places *en route*. Opposite Clayton, on the left, as we proceed down the river, is Governor Island, owned by Hon. Thomas G. Alvord, of Syracuse. Next to Gov. Alvord's Isle, on the left, is Calumet, five acres, owned by Chas. G. Emery, of Old Judge cigarette and tobacco fame, who has lavishly expended a large amount of money for comfort. His villa and apartments are quite striking, having 1,000 feet of dockage and a stone wall all around the island, 4,300 feet—the only island having an elevation of 35 feet and a perfect soil, all productive. He purchased the steam yacht "Calumet," said to be one of the fastest yachts on the river. The next island on the left, about 200 yards distant, is Powder Horn. The origin of this "euphonious" name has not been handed down by tradition. On the right is Washington Island; on the left nearly opposite, is Bluff Island; behind which is Robin's Island. Next on the right over two miles from Clayton, is

ROUND ISLAND

and park. This is the property of the Baptist Association, and every year people of this persuasion, in large numbers, gather for religious worship and recreation. There is a hotel, fitted up with the modern appointments, for the accommodation of 300 guests, named the "Hotel Frontenac," which opens June 27th this year and will remain throughout the month of September. This hotel has always been patronized by the better class of tourists and Thousand Island visitors. This season it will be under the able management of C. W. MacAvoy, and I am positive, after looking up his record as a hotel man, you cannot regret making a stay at the Frontenac. Docks are in excellent condition, and the fishing boats are favorites. On the left is Little Round Island and "Hog's Back." We have now several cottages in view; the one painted dark brown is owned by Mr. Harbodle. On the point is Ethelridge cottage, and many others not known to me, as they spring up as quickly as mushrooms do in an open field.

Leaving Round Island, and looking in the distant front, we have a view of the Thousand Island Park. About one mile from Round Island, on the right, is

Watch Island or "Indolence," owned by S. T. Skinner. On the left are Bluff, Maple and Hemlock, the three pretty islands fronting the foot of Grindstone Island. On Hemlock is the Cliff House, owned by Mr. Garrison, of Syracuse. The island has been purchased by the 1,000 Island Investment Company and is called Murray Hill Park. This energy displayed if kept up will soon make this the spot among the 1,000 Islands. About five minutes after leaving Round Island, we come on the left in sight of Hub Island. A large hotel, the Hub House, occupied this sight, but was burned in March, 1884; Grinnell's Island and Pullman House; Otsego Camp is also on the left. On the right is Fisher's landing, Robinson's Island, owned by Eugene Robinson, New York, banker and broker, (he broke Drew). This island was purchased by W. C. McCord of New York. Johnson's Light, Washburn Island and Frederick Island. Mr. Johnson, the original light-house keeper, and after whom the island is named, was the man who burned the "Robert Peel," the English vessel in retaliation for sending the "Caroline" over Niagara Falls.

Just before landing at Thousand Island Park, upper end of Wells Island, is Twin Island, owned by J. L. Huntington. Also Castle "Fannie" Chase owned by the Rev. W. Demster Chase, of New York. On the left, and in connection with the Thousand Island Park, is the bath house, (in a dilapidated condition), where the Methodists formerly received baptism, *a la* Bob Ingersoll, with soap. Said to be good for this world, if not hereafter. We now land at

THOUSAND ISLAND PARK.

The boat stops at the western end of Wells Island, at a fine wharf and close to a large number of handsome cottages. You can tell what the place is the minute you approach it. There is no mistaking a Methodist Summer Camp, find it where you will. It is always neat and clean and orderly. This is the Thousand Island Park, a Methodist resort, opened in 1873. Although the scenery is somewhat marred by the great number of solemn-faced clergymen strolling about the grounds, it is still one of the most beautiful spots to be found among the islands. Camp meetings are held here ; also Sunday school and temperance and educational conventions, and other meetings all through the summer. A large and spacious hotel was opened July 10th, 1883, and was destroyed by fire in August, 1890. It was rebuilt last season and will be open sometime in July. The name was originally Thousand Island Camp ground, but was changed in 1878 to its present name.

Again on our way, the first house on the left is owned by Harlow J. Remington, of Ilion, N. Y., whose fame and fortune are in Rifles. The Island fronting the Bay was purchased by Messrs. Ocumpaugh and Furman, two of Rochester's favorite business men. It contains about thirty building lots. I hope soon to see several fine cottages erected thereon. Next on the left is Fine View House and beautiful cottage. On the left, handsome villas line the shore of the island. About half a mile from Fine View House is Jolly Oak Point with its four cottages, two owned by the Norton brothers, a third by Dr. Ferguson, and the fourth by Hon. W. W. Butterfield, of Redwood. From here to Lookout Point is about half a mile ; and next is Rood's place, with a fine dock and good accommodations for tourists. About two hundred yards below is Peel's dock, where the boat "Robert Peel" was burned in 1837. This dock was

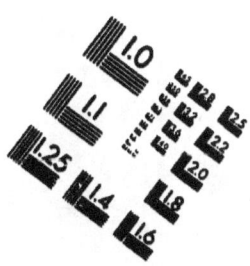

IMAGE EVALUATION
TEST TARGET (MT-3)

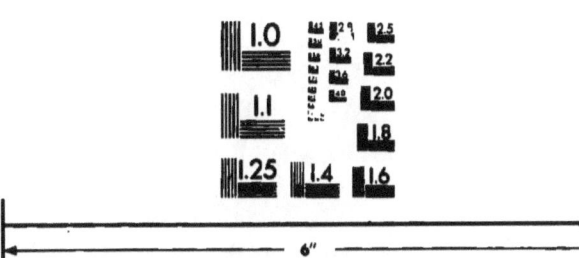

Photographic
Sciences
Corporation

23 WEST MAIN STREET
WEBSTER, N.Y. 14580
(716) 872-4503

rebuilt in 1884. Robin's cottage, one hundred feet to the left, is Island Blanch, owned by E. D. Buckingham ; a little below on the right is the farm of Captain Jack ; you can see the old saw-mill in a dilapidated condition on the bank. Opposite on the left is the celebrated Limburger cheese factory. (Post mortem examination held here weekly.) (This " goak " would take better if you were just introduced to Limburger for the first time.) On the right is Collins' dock ; below, a few feet, is Calumet Island and cottage, owned by Oliver H. Green, No. 6 Calumet court, Boston, Mass. On the right lies the remains of old Captain Jack's Boat gone to rest. * * * * Here you are expected to drop a tear. Brown's Bay on the left and Swan Bay on the right. The next island on the right is owned by Harrison Stillman and is named St. Helena, and has a very fine representation of the tomb of Napoleon. Passing the bays, we come on the right to Central Park, formerly Grinnel's Point and parade ground, purchased by parties and laid out for a park. Several large and beautiful cottages were built last season and many contemplated for this season. On the left opposite on the bluff, is Hill's Crest, owned by General Shields, of Philadelphia, Pa. Foot of Central Park is Page Point, a former wood station for the N. T. Co's line of steamers. On the right is

POINT VIVIAN.

Point Vivian is situated on the main shore of the St. Lawrence River, about two and one-half miles from Alexandria Bay. It was formerly owned by Captain W. H. Houghton, and was purchased by Messrs. George Ivers, John J. Kinney, Isaac A. Wood, Dr. L.

E. Jones, R. Barnes, Rezot Tozer, and E. Hungerford, in the fall of 1877 (all of Evans Mills, N. Y.). They had it surveyed into forty building lots, with parks, avenues and streets. A magnificent dock was built two hundred feet long, and any boat from a skiff to an ocean steamer can land here.

Opposite point Vivian on the left is Island Royal, owned by Royal E. Deane, of New York, firm of Bramall, Deane & Co. Mr. Deane is a very enthusiastic lover of the scenery as well as the hunting and fishing in this vicinity, coming to this, his summer home, quite early in the spring, and often remaining until winter fairly sets in, for nowhere else can he get such a variety of fish and game, and have the surroundings so agreeable. Next on the left is Shady Covert, owned by Editor J. C. Covert of the *Cleveland Leader*.

After leaving Point Vivian, on the right is Curtice Point and Cottage, which joins Rose Island by a bridge. Here is where Mayor W. G. Rose, of Cleveland Ohio, enjoys his summers. The next is Allegheny Point, owned by J. S. Laney, of Pittsburgh, Pa. The fence was built to keep the children from falling into the river. Opposite on the left is Seven Isles, owned by General Bradley Winslow. Next on the right is Ritter's Heights owned by Mr. Frank Ritter, of Rochester, N. Y., beyond is Keppler Point, Bella Vista Lodge, owned by F. A. Bosworth, of Milwaukee, Wis. This property, Bella Vista Lodge, was sold to Mr. R. B. Chisholm, of Cleveland, O. Centennial, now Nah-Mahbin, meaning Twin Island or Lakes, is owned by Mr. J. H. Oliphant, of Brooklyn, N. Y. Comfort, in close proximity, is owned by A. E. Clark. of the Chicago, Ill., Board of Trade. His is the largest and finest cottage of the group.

Next is H. H. Warner's Island, upon which $50,000 has been expended in the erection of his new cottage. Beyond this is Hill's Island. This gentleman has expended a large amount of money in building a stone wall around the same and in many ways beautifying the surroundings. Next on the right is Devil's Rock and Oven—owned by H. R. Heath, of New York. On the left is Louisiana Point, owned by Judge LeBatte, of New Orleans. Next on the left is Craig's Side, owned by H. A. Laughin, of Pittsburgh, Pa. On the right is Cuba Isle, owned by W. F. Storey, of Buffalo, N. Y. A little farther on is Edgewood Park, owned by a Cleveland stock company who erected an elegant hotel, which was opened in 1887, and contemplate many changes the coming season ; also Edgewood Cottage, owned by G. C. Martin, of Watertown, N. Y. Next on the right is Cherry Isle, upon which are erected several cottages ; the first is owned by the Rev. George Rockwell, of Fulton, N. Y. ; and J. T. Easton's Villa, of Brooklyn. N. Y. Mr. Easton, of Brooklyn, erected a handsome villa, called Stuyvesant Cottage, which he occupied during the season. The two large cottages are owned by A. B. Pullman and C. B. Marsh, of Chicago, Ill., named Ingleside and Melrose Lodge. Here the Hon. John A. Logan and wife were entertained for several days in 1885. Opposite on the left is "The Towers," owned by Mr. W. C. Browning, of Browning, King & Co., New York, Pullman, Nobby, Friendly, St. Elmo, Welcome, Florence, Linlithgow and Imperial. This group may be seen in the order given ; beyond is Westminster Park, Hart's Island, Fairy Land and Deshler. We now shoot into

ALEXANDRIA BAY,

which is three or four miles long and one and a half miles wide, reaching from the shore on the American side to Wells Island. The chief feature around here is the grand hotels. The Crossmon House, and Thousand Island House are the two largest hotels and being situated on the river front give the guests a delightful view.

WESTMINSTER PARK.

Opposite Alexandria Bay on the lower end of Wells Island. This island is eight miles long and from three to four miles wide. On the other side of this island is the Canadian channel of the river, about half a mile wide. The lower end of the island is separated into two parts by one of the prettiest sheets of water that ever rippled against the bows of a canoe. This is called the "Lake of the Island," and is connected with the river on both the American and Canadian sides by a narrow channel. The lake is five or six miles long, as smooth as glass, and is altogether too pretty and too romantic to attempt a description.

Westminster Park was bought in 1874 by a Presbyterian stock company, and it now has about fifteen miles of drives and some fine buildings. It has two long water fronts—one on the American side of the river and the other on the Lake of the Island, on the Canadian side. There is a high hill on the island called Mount Beulah, though after climbing it I think the Hill Difficulty would be a more appropriate name. There is a large chapel on the top of the hill, known as Bethune Chapel, with seating accommodations for a thousand persons, and with a tower 136 feet high, (was blown down in March, 1885). The name of the chapel recalls the fact that the late Rev. Dr. Geo. W. Bethune was the poineer tourist through this region, who until his death continued to come here summer after summer for recreation. A new church is now being erected a short distance from the hotel.

BONNIE CASTLE.

"Timothy Titcomb" (Dr. J. G. Holland, editor o *Scribner's Monthly*), chose this place as a haven of rest and recuperation, and who does not commend his choice? It will be remembered that he died in New York shortly after leaving his cherished Bonnie Castle in 1881, for his arduous winter's labors. Next is The Ledges, owned by C. J. Hudson, of New York. Lighthouse in the distance.

Immediately opposite is Hart's Island; back of which is Deshler. Next on the left is

MANHATTAN,

the first island on which habitation was attempted. It was bought by Mr. Seth Green, the fish culturist of N.Y., in 1855. He built a cottage upon it and for several years spent his summers here. Mr. J. L. Hasbrouck and Judge J. C. Spencer, of New York, purchased it from him. They have spent $15,000 upon the island. The original cottages built by Seth Green still remain and are used by them as dining rooms, etc. Beyond is St. John's Island, owned by Judge Donohue, of New York.

Between Deshler and Manhattan, looking backward, is Fairyland, owned by C. H. and W. B. Hayden, of

Columbus, Ohio. This is really one of the finest islands in the river. At a vast expense art has triumphed over nature, transforming a barren into the loveliest of green lawns. Next on the left is Deer Island ; then

SUMMERLAND.

Summerland, one of the most beautiful groups of the " Thousand Islands," is located mid-way between the north and south channels of the St. Lawrence, about three miles below Alexandria Bay, having an area of fourteen acres, and is the largest of the "Summerland group," which includes " Idlewild, " " Sport, " "Ida, " and " Arcadia." The island is covered with a dense forest (furnishing an abundance of shade) and is said to have the finest groves on the river. At the extreme northerly and southerly ends of the Island there are extensive sand beaches, a great rarity in this locality, which are used by the " Summerlanders " for bathing purposes. The island is traversed from end to end by the most delightful natural avenue, densely shaded and lined on either side with a thick undergrowth of wild flowers and ferns. The island is owned by the Summerland Association, a corporation organized under and by virtue of the laws of the State of New York.

Between Deer Island and Summerland is Cedar ; back of Cedar is Sport, owned by the estate of H. A. Packer, who died in 1884. The island, however, will be occupied this year by E. P. Wilbur, who has purchased the Packers' interest. Anthony point is on the right. Also The Ledges, owned by J. C. Hudson, of New York.

Still continuing our course looking to the right, is the cottage of Mrs. Clark, of Watertown. Next, Goose Bay is the island owned by Dr. Carleton, near which is the Three Sisters' Island ; before the Three Sisters is Hume's Island. Next, on the left, is Whiskey Island, and on the right, opposite, are a number of large and small islands, the names of which we will not weary the tourist's brain with.

Goose Bay is really beautiful, if its name is slightly homely. It is studded with islands and fishing abounds. It is here that Mr. Hubert R. Clark, of New York, in one day caught some 300 pounds of black bass, ranging in weight from 1½ to 6½ pounds.

On the right is Lyon's dock and Meeker's Island. Next, on the left is Three Sisters Light ; in the distance is Lone Star, or Dark Island ; island No. 10, it is called by some. After passing, on the left is a small cluster of island shoals. On the right is Chippewa Bay. This is a superb sheet of water, where the fishing is a marked feature. It is a favorite resort of Ogdensburg people, who occupy the contiguous islands. This property, "Chippewa Point" and Allen's Park and dock, has been purchased by a wealthy syndicate who propose erecting a commodious hotel and each member building for his own use a handsome villa. I look to see this the grandest resort among the Thousand Islands. All around the shore are camps, cottages, etc., and make an animated scene for the tourist.

After passing Cross-over Light, and before reaching Cole's Light, we come in sight of Union Park. It was formerly a Methodist camp ground. It has been purchased by a Scotch syndicate, who erected a large hotel and many pretty cottages. Villas, camps, and cottages line the shore until we arrive at Gallenas Place. This was built for the purpose of having a resort for "*a class*" I am glad to say do not thrive on the St. Lawrence.

Places where liquor parties, drunken sprees and such like have been started many times on this river, but have been short lived.

Hill Crest comes first, then Fern Bank, formerly McDonald's Point, with St. Lawrence Park on main land, Crossitt's Agricultural Works; McCullough; Jno. F. Wood; Bowie; Parker Wilkinson; Greenmore and Kincade. Then we come in sight of R. B. Hather's flower and fruit farm, his fine windmill and boat-house on the river bank. This gentleman supplies the Thousand Islanders and guests at the hotels with flowers. He is recognized as the florist of the St. Lawrence River. A Hather buttonhole bouquet is quite necessary to complete one's toilet, and many times has the author of this book become the admiration of many on account of the large bouquet which adorned his huge but magnificent physique. The next on the left is Smith's Island, owned by R. H. Smart, a hardware merchant of Brockville. On the main shore beyond is River Cliff and many pretty villas, including Bay View, Cole's Island on the left, and McLean's cottage. Just before reaching Brockville, is H. A. Field's and Geo. A. Dana's residence.

In front of Brockville are the last three of the Thousand Islands; being some distance from the rest it is presumable they drifted away, and finally rooted here. This, however, was "long befo' de wah!"

Opposite, on the right, is Morristown, a small lively American village of about 1,000 inhabitants, a station on the Utica and Black River R. R., connects with Brockville by two steam ferries.

BROCKVILLE

was named in honor of General Brock, who fell in the battle of Queenstown Heights in 1812. It is situated on the Canadian side of the St. Lawrence River, and is one of the pleasantest villages in the Province. It lies at the foot of the Thousand Islands on an elevation of land which rises from the river in a succession of ridges. The town was laid out in 1802, and is now a place of considerable importance. The present population is about 10,000.

After leaving the wharf, the boat passes the most beautiful cliff on the river, the Palisades of the St. Lawrence, on which are erected magnificent mansions and suburban residences and villas of Canada's distinguished sons. The most prominent of these is the son of Sir Hugh Allen, whose residence is really supurb. The sightseer can observe the winding stairs, boat and bath houses and other appointments for recreation.

Having left Brockville, a magnificent view greets the eye; islands are not now in view; the river is a most beautiful sheet of water, running perfectly straight for about sixteen miles with the land on either side in good view, for the river is a little over two miles wide. Three miles from Morristown, on the right, is a camp ground of the Baptist persuasion, mostly from St. Lawrence County. Five miles on the left from Brockville is Maitland. At this point is a prominent object known as the old distillery, whose proprietor is said to have been worth at one time, a million dollars, but whose cupidity during "America's unpleasantness" led him into selling "crooked whiskey," or rather disposing of his distillery products in a very "crooked" way. Without going into the details, the facts in brief are : He antagonized the Canadian government in the matter of paying revenue, and in his fight for stupid supremacy, he not only lost his distillery, but his fortune too, and he and his family became reduced to poverty, and none of them remain around their former home. It is said he first induced his niece to marry the revenue collector of the district, that he might carry on the nefarious business in collusion and without detection, but you see

" The deep laid plans of mice and men gang aft aglee."

About four miles below, on the left, is the old blue stone church, in the graveyard of which rests the remains of the founder of Methodism on this continent, Barbara Heck. One mile further, on the left, is McCarthy's new brick brewery. Half a mile beyond is the celebrated Rysdick stock farm, owned by J.P.Wiser, M. P. Here is owned the celebrated stallion Rysdick, which cost Mr. Wiser $25,000. It is a farm of about six hundred acres, and is unquestionably the finest stock farm in the dominion of Canada. The thrift, energy and ability of this gentleman will not be wondered at when it is learned that he is of American birth. Next, on the left, is the celebrated Labatt's brewery and

PRESCOTT,

with its nearly 3,000 inhabitants, who seem to have lost their grip on the trade of the river, judging from the dilapidated condititon of the stores, warehouses, etc., on the wharves. The town, however, is handsomely laid out, has a fine city hall and market and new postoffice, and there are many fine private residences. It is connected with Ottawa, capital of the Dominion, by the

Canada Pacific Railroad, St. Lawrence and Ottawa Railroad Branch, distance 54 miles. Here many tourists who desire to visit the capital disembark for that purpose. We refer the tourists to Daniels' hotel as a good stopping place. L. H. Daniels has taken the hotel and spent $8,000 in improvements; he is too well known to the traveling public to need any praise from me. Opposite is

OGDENSBURG,

founded by Francis Picquit in May, 1749. It now contains about 15,000 people, and of course ranks as a city. It is the terminus of the Rome and Watertown, Utica and Black River, and the Ogdensburg and Lake Champlain railroads. It is beautifully laid out, well planted with maple trees, and is called the "Maple City." It has a United States Custom House, postoffice, and a new opera house, costing $15,000, six fine church edifices, water works, gas works, a fire alarm telegraph and two daily newspapers, and possibly other modern improvements. Here the Oswegatchie River empties into the St. Lawrence; its waters are of a dark brown color. At the lower end of the town are the big elevators of the Ogdensburg and Lake Champlain Railroad, now owned by the Central Vermont Railroad. Many tourists start from here in the morning, reaching every point in the White Mountains before tea time.

One mile and a half below Prescott on the left, is Windmill Pcint; the old windmill has been turned into a lighthouse. Here, in 1838, the "Patriots," under Von Schultz, a Polish exile, established themselves, but from which they were driven with severe loss. Mr. C. Crossmon, proprietor of the Crossmon House, Alexandria Bay, N. Y. one of the "Patriots," was taken prisoner and for several days took his chances with the thirteen selected to be shot, but before his time came he was released on account of his tender years, being only 16 years old. He is looking hale and hearty to-day for one so young. We believe this Von Schultz was subsequently hung by the Canadian authorities, and his followers banished, probably to New Jersey. On the left, a little below the lighthouse, is the residence and farm of W. H. McGannon, the oldest pilot on the St. Lawrence river, the man who first took the "Passport," of the Richelieu line, down the Long Sault Rapids, in July, 1847. I am also indebted to him for the correctness of my New Map of the St. Lawrence and other information of benefit to me and the public.

About half a mile below, on the right, the eye may feast on the St. Lawrence State Hospital for the Insane in process of erection. About one half a million dollars was secured by General Curtis for the enterprise, and if carried out as projected, this will be the finest grounds and hospital in the country.

Three miles below, on the left, is Johnstown Bay, with Johnstown—not a very important trading post—overlooking. This place has a custom house officer, commissioner of fisheries, mayor and marshal of the district; but these important officials are concentrated in one man.

We turn here to the right, leaving the far-famed Chimney Island on the left, on which are said to be the remains of old French forts, battlements, etc. The only ruins we have discovered of these supposed formidable defences is an extensive moat around the island, twelve feet deep, filled with water. The chimney, from which it derives its name, is supposed to be on the island, but we have looked in vain to discover it. It may be, however, that it has floated down the river; we will speak of it further on.

In the distance, on the left, are Tick or Pier Islands. Some of the finest bass fishing in the river is off this old pier. Dr. Melville, of Prescott, the inventor of rheumatic victor, and an enthusiastic fisherman of this section, last summer caught a black bass weighing seven and one-half pounds while enjoying the sport around the pier.

Three miles from Chimney Island, in the distance is what is termed "the cut," forming the channel between Galop and Moore's Islands. It was the former channel of this line of boats, but the Dominion government is expending six millions of dollars for the enlargement of the canals of this route, and the survey party at present are blasting a channel through the

GALOP RAPID,

which may be seen in the distance. The reason of the change of channel is formed with an edict of the pilots not to interfere with the work of the engineer corps engaged on this necessary improvement of excavating a fifteen foot channel, to allow larger boats to pass, and dispense with the use of the Edwardsburg canal. After five years of waiting and trying to accomplish their purpose, the scheme of blasting out the channel was dispensed with and a portion of the canal was enlarged as the current in the river was too strong for boats to come up. This is the first and smallest rapid on the St. Lawrence river, and as the Phat Boy has termed it, "a little one for a cent." I will, however, give you an idea of what the rapids are. All the rapids on this river are caused by numerous rocks, large and small, in the bed of the river, and the swift current of water passing over these rocks, causes the fearful commotion that you observe. Now, to carry our philosophy a little farther, we say the larger the rock and the stronger the current the better the rapids. No rocks, no water, no current, no rapids ! This commotion which you see here is caused by a ledge of rocks, five and one-half feet in height under nine feet of water. You can see the swell and white cap which this rock occasions, and then use your best judgment to determine the height of the rocks in Long Sault, where we hope to arrive at one o'clock. (There are, let me state here, eight rapids on our trip to-day, which may be divided into two classes, first and second. The first class are Long Sault, meaning a long leap or jump ; Cedar, deriving its name from the trees in the vicinity, and Lachine. The second class is Galop, meaning a hopping, jumping rapid ; Rapid Platt, meaning in French flat ; Chateau du Lac, meaning foot of the lake ; Split Rock, derived from a fissure which makes the channel, and the Cascade, from its resemblance to a cascade).

On the left, before arriving at the Galop Rapids, is the entrance to the Edwardsburg canal. This canal is seven and one-half miles in length, and is the first canal we arrive at ; its terminus is at Iroquois. It would be well here to say that we only have canals around the rapids, or where the current is too strong for a steamer to ascend. We here append a tabular statement of the

ST. LAWRENCE CANALS.

Edwardsburg canal 7½ miles long, three locks, 14 feet fall in the river ; Morrisburg canal, 4 miles long, 2 locks, 11⅙ feet fall ; Farrhn's Point canal ¾ mile long, 1 lock, 4 feet fall ; Cornwall canal, 12 miles long, 7 locks, 48 feet fall ; Beauharnois canal 11½, miles long, 9 locks, 84 feet fall ; Lachine canal, 9 miles long, 5 locks, 45 feet fall.

In the distance, on the left, is the village of Edwardsburg, now called Cardinal. Here is located the Edwardsburg starch factory, the largest in the Dominion of Canada. The president of the Company is the Hon. Walter Shanley of Hoosac Tunnel fame. He was the great contractor who completed that wonderful piece of work, and was manager of the St. Lawrence and Ottawa Railroad.

Twenty minutes from Edwardsburg to the next point of interest.

Distinguished among Indian names is that of Iroquois. Here it names a village, formerly known as Matilda ; but, like all other good Matildas do, she changed her name to Iroquois, in order to preserve the name. The Iroquois Indians formerly owned this section of country. One and a half miles below this village, is the narrowest point in the St. Lawrence River, from Kingston to the gulf. This broad expanse of water we are just passing, and the one we arrive at immediately after leaving the point, are very shallow, consequently holds the water in check at the point—the depth of water in the shallow places being about 22 feet while at the point it is 84 feet. Width of the river 1,140 feet—180 feet less than a quarter of a mile.

On the right in the narrowest portion of the river is Cedar Point. On the left is a small bluff, formerly called Hemlock Point, on account of a fine hemlock standing there ; but on one fine morning the hemlock, the tree and the point all slid into the river, and have not yet returned. About fifteen feet back from the point is a rail fence, which is outside of the earth works that were thrown up in 1812-13, and batteries were erected on Cedar Point.

On the left is the main shore of the Dominion of Canada with a population of over six millions. On the right is the main shore of the United States of America, with a population of over sixty millions. When the six millions want the sixty millions all they will be obliged to do is to walk over and take them. Then will be verified that beautiful passage in Holy Writ which says, "One shall chase a thousand and two put ten thousand to flight." Sing!

This was really a strong point, and was fortified on both sides of the river by the opposing parties. From the fact of the successful fortification by the Americans the Rideau Canal owes its origin. Guns and stores or merchandise could not be taken up the river. It was conceived by Colonel By, of the engineer corps, that a new canal would obviate the difficulty, and all his resources were immediately put into requisition, and the canal was completed at a cost of $5,000,000. It extends from Ottawa, formerly By-town, to Kingston, and is still in use.

Ten minutes from here to the next point of interest. On the left is the entrance to the Morrisburg Canal, the second canal in the chain, but it is not used by this line of boats. All tows and sailing vessels have to use the canals. In the distant front is rapid Platt : on the right is Ogden's Island, the finest wooded Island in the St. Lawrence. Beyond is Waddington, St. Lawrence County, N. Y. In front is this rapid we have just named ; it is the second one, and is "a little one for two cents." It has, however, eight feet more descent than the first, but is only a one cent *descenter* rapid.

MORRISBURG.

After passing the point, Morrisburg comes into view on the left—the prettiest village in the Dominion of Canada. Look at its churches, public buildings, private residences, and hotels (the St. Lawrence Hall is kept by W. H. McCannon, and I can say cheerfully no better hotel in town), that greet the eye, for we are still in the Province of Ontario. At half past three o'clock we enter the Province of Quebec. You will have a good chance then to compare the two provinces. Your especial attention is called to this now, that you may be prepared to scan the change you will not fail to observe. Before reaching Morrisburg is Doran's Island, which was rented by Mr. Oz Doran of the St. Regis Indians for one dollar per year, and they come every year 60 miles to collect one dollar. A railroad bridge was to have been completed at this point during the present year. Opposite Morrisburg is Dry Island, used for picnics, etc.

One hour from this point to the Long Sault Rapids. We speak of this here, for it is about dinner time, and if you are lucky enough to secure a seat at the first table you will lose no point of interest, for it is presumable you will finish within the hour.

THE CUISINE ON THE BOAT.

It will not be amiss here to state that the meals were formerly served on the American plan, in the upper saloon, and to give you but a faint idea of the commotion created by the passengers when there was one more person on board than seats at the table, would require a volume ten times this size to describe. Therefore, please excuse me if I relate by way of illustration what an eminent writer said on the subject : " The waiters, like little puppets, would bob up serenely at any time and place, drop a dish or whatever the hand contained, and were as soon out of sight. This continued for about one hour, while we were seated back against the cabin wall, with just space enough for the waiter to pass between us and the table. When the signal was given everybody made a rush for the table, and if the scene depicted could only be described, humorously or otherwise, I would like to read it." But the writer said it reminded him of the famous picture in her Majesty's gallery, " The rape of the Sabines." (I have never seen the picture, but presume it is that of a beautiful female poised as a central figure, and about ten soldiers ready to embrace her on a given signal.) Things have changed, however, and this season the meals will be served on the American plan, run by the company, who have secured the best stewards, etc., to superintend the service, to the end that everyone may be pleased. The upper saloon will not be used, but what was formerly known as the ladies' cabin, and the cabin below, has been refitted, containing ample table room for everybody, and will be the dining rooms ; there have also been added a new kitchen, steam tables, etc., which gives the whole saloon as a promenade and place of rest and repose for the passengers. I am positive the change will be acceptable.

About a mile below Morrisburg, on the right, is Gooseneck Island, so called from its resemblance to the neck of a goose ; the upper end is the neck ; the narrative is about nine miles long. Five miles from Morrisburg to

CHRYSLER'S FARM,

memorable for the battle fought on this ground in the year 1813. The Americans were the attacking party on this occasion, having arisen early in the morning, crossed the river into the little bay, landed and immediately gone into the contest by attacking the little house. The fight was desperate, lasting until eleven o'clock, when the Americans, under General Williams, were repulsed with great slaughter. The house was completely riddled with bullets. It has since been torn down and the chimney left as a monument to the battle. They retreated in good order, re-crossed the river and remained, having abandoned the trip to Montreal which they intended. I draw this mild because I am one of " God's people " myself.

Next in interest is Farron's Point, opposite which is Croyl's Island. Six minutes from here to Long Sault rapids ; we pass on the left Harrison's Landing.

LONG SAULT ISLAND.

At this point there are really two channels, the American Channel being on the right of Long Sault Island, the rapids forming the Canadian channel, and are on the left of the Island. The distinguishing feature about the American Channel is, while it is swift in current, it has no rapids worthy of note, and the channel is used for tows, etc., and all the rafts naturally prefer this way, because it would be impossible for them to go down the Long Sault.

In the distant front observe a light-house at the head of the Cornwall canal. The canal is twelve miles in length, and passes around the Long Sault Rapids.

The boats are steered from landmarks on the shore by that small ball you see on the end of the pole, which is the bow-sprit. The target that you see in the distance is used by the pilot to get his position in Long Sault Rapids. These targets will be seen frequently as you progress, and as they all answer the same purpose, this reference to them will suffice.

LONG SAULT RAPIDS.

Dickinson's Landing, on the left, was formerly a very important point on this line, as it was the foot of navigation before the canal was completed, some forty years ago. Few changes have taken place since, that are apparent to the eye. The Long Sault is the first one of the first-class rapids, and the third one in line proceeding down the river, and as we set a price on the other two you can set your own price on this one. A description of these rapids has been given from time immemorial; it does not behoove us to give any graphic or colored description of this scene, although we might do so satisfactorily, having seen depicted on the countenances of thousands of passengers who have passed this way everything in nature, from the sublime to the ridiculous, as well as between the two, and as each individual's feelings differ, no one description would do the subject justice. One writer said: "It was sliding down hill on a steam-boat." Another said he felt as if he was being *unglued!* A third said he felt as if he had taken a large dose of ipecac. Still another, as if he was on a ship at sea in a storm. And yet one more was so exhilarated that he imagined he owned Maud S. and would like to spend his days on the rapids. Another party who had ridiculed the trip a good deal, until the spray began to cover the deck, wetting them to the skin, drenching their store clothes, which, when dried revealed awkward misfits, exclaimed that "it was the grandest sight they ever witnessed."

I could enlarge upon other descriptions, but prefer to give the Phat Boy a privilege to relate a few facts—no "taffy." All the boats of this line are built of Bessemer steel or iron, with three and one-half inches of elm riveted close to the iron on the bottom outside to prevent accidents if we should strike against a rock. This precaution was found necessary, because the first iron boat that struck a rock became a total wreck. With the protection of elm no injury has resulted from the occasional striking of the boats against the rocks. There is no danger, however, in this rapid, for the water in the shallowest place is thirteen and one-half feet and we are drawing about seven feet. During our passage through all the rapids, we have four men at the wheel and four men at the tiller aft, who assist the men at the wheel. Any accident that should happen to the chain or the wheel, the pilot immediately goes to the right hand of the tiller.

The Long Sault Rapid is nine miles long ; three miles of boisterous commotion ; six miles of current and sudden sharp turns. When we first enter the rapid the steam on board of the boat is slowed down until she gets her position in the rapids, as she draws less water than when under full head of steam. We are then compelled to put on full steam as the boat must go faster than the current in order to obtain steerage way. Many suppose that no steam is used through the rapids, which is an error. If we were to attempt to go down without any propelling power, we would be at the mercy of the current of this stupendous agitation called rapids. One couldn't tell which end of the boat would be first, and it is presumable that this would be anything but pleasant to the passenger, for she would go down the same as a log; no one could tell which end of the boat would be first--anything but pleasure to the passengers.

When we first enter this rapid the finest view is obtained on the right side of the boat. It is expected however, that the passengers will distribute themselves equally on either side to keep the boat in good trim— the captain generally uses the "Phat Boy" for this purpose; when he is not on board the passengers are expected to distribute themselves. The view, however soon changes to the left, and when nearing the point the swell and white caps run from seven to eleven feet in height.

We have already explained the cause of the rapids. Now, will anyone please explain to me what is the height of the rocks which create this commotion, and at the same time set their price on this rapid? After passing this point and the swell and white caps that we have been describing, on the left is the passage to the Canadian channel of this river, which forms Barnhardt's Island. On the right is the American channel. This was formerly used by boats before they came down the Long Sault, which for a long time was known as the lost channel. This channel having been lost for some years, it was discovered by Captain Rankin, who received for that service a magnificent silver watch, the value of which at the present day would be about $6.50. The first steamboat of this line that passed through the Long Sault, was the " Passport " (1890 the " New Passport " took her place in the line), in 1847, and the pilot was W. H. McGannon, who is still in the employ of the company. The soundings were made by scows and rafts, with poles attached to the sides, of 8 to 15 feet in length, and as either of these met an obstruction and became dislodged or broken off, the depth of the water was ascertained and a record made. The propelling power of these scows or rafts was oars or large paddles, worked by from 10 to 40 men as the necessities of each required.

The steamer "Gill" was the first boat through the rapids, and went down more by accident than otherwise, but it demonstrated the certainty of a channel.

Barnhardt's Island, on the left, 7½ miles in length by 4½ miles in width, belongs to the United States. On the right is the main land, St. Lawrence County, N. Y. Both sides of the river for the next seven miles belong to the United States. The King of Holland, who was the arbitrator of the treaty of 1812, from charts, maps, etc., furnished him, supposed that the main channel of the river passed around that Island on the left. He was mistaken however; this is the main channel of the river, and the only navigable one, the Canadian channel containing only about 3½ or 4 feet of water.

During the next eight minutes we pass three very sudden turns in the river; the first turn is to the right, then to the left; next to the right again; the second turn being the sharpest on the St. Lawrence River; at direct angles turning to the left. Passengers on the left side of the boat, by looking backward, have a fine view of that portion of the river we have just passed, and looking forward see where we are compelled to go, and more easily note the sharpness of the turn. Rafts entering the American channel at the foot of the Long Sault rapids will drift nine miles in forty minutes, and are often thrown on shore on either side in making this sudden turn. After making our next turn to the right, by looking in the distance, front, between the narrow point, we discover what is known as "The Crab." The current crosses here from right to left, then left to right, and from right to left, forming the letter Z. Rafts get entangled in this portion of the river, and are easily torn to pieces.

There is a ferry boat plying between this point, on the right, Macenia Point and Cornwall Point on the left, touching at two places on Barnhardt's Island, to convey passengers who are desirous of visiting Macenia Springs, six miles distant. The steamboat is a side-wheeler, two horses tread the power that revolves the wheels; it is therefore a two-horse boat; they convey the steam on board in a bag well filled with oats. The deck hand is the cook; the cook is the engineer; the engineer is the mate, and the mate is the captain; one man supreme commands; no mutiny ever occurs, unless the mule should kick the deck hand overboard—that would be a "*mulity*," would it not?

On the left is the entrance to the Canadian channel at the end of Barnhardt's Island. Two miles below on the right is the last of the American shore on the St. Lawrence, lat. 45° N. Some few years ago I was presented by one of the firms in the city, with an American flag fifteen feet in length, to designate the last of the United States shore on this river. Through the assistance of a friend at Cornwall, and thirteen dollars in cash, I succeeded in getting the flag in position. It remained there for about ten days, when a party of St. Regis Indians, who occupy a reservation six miles distant, the other side of the river—four of them came over to the point, filled themselves full of "ice water," climbed up the flag-staff and took down the flag. They cut it up into three or four suits of clothes, and went around this vicinity for about a week as full as a boiled oyster, singing "Hail Columbia, right side up," rolled up in the stars and stripes, full of fire water ; it was said to be the happiest moment of their lives, and I have no reason to doubt it. On June 7th, 1887, I was presented by Mr. S. Carsley, the leading dry goods merchant of Montreal, with another splendid American flag, and I hope when placed in position it may wave until I cease issuing this little volume, and on white wings, etc., etc.

That portion of the river on the right is the dividing line for five miles ; afterwards an iron fence, or posts set at equal distance apart, mark the boundary line. The river passing around that way forms Cornwall Island, about six miles wide. Rafts enter this portion of the river where the Racket river empties in, and are here refitted preparatory to being towed through the lake. Both sides of the river from this point downward belong to the Dominion of Canada.

In the distance, on the left is Cornwall, a village of 8,000 people, with the largest cotton and woolen mills, in the Dominion. Since the protective tariff was inaugurated by the Dominion Parliament, these industries have thrived wonderfully, and the town is correspondingly prosperous. The large round tower is the water works reservoir. Just before landing a fine view is obtained of both the old and new Cornwall canals. Looking at the old canal lock, and learning its dimensions, it is obvious why the steamers are the limit which the locks will admit, hence if they were five feet longer or a trifle wider, they would be compelled to remain at Montreal, not being able to work through the locks. The new canal which is alongside of the old one, will have locks 100 feet longer than the present ones in use, consequently much larger boats will be able to ply the river. The old canal was considered amply large when built ; it was not supposed that the travel on the St. Lawrence would ever reach its present and constantly increasing numbers.

After leaving Cornwall, on the right is Cornwall Island, six miles wide. Just beyond the Island, on the right bank of the river, is St. Regis, an old Indian village, which cannot be seen from the deck of the steamer. But there is just one point where the church roof can be observed for a moment or so. There is, however, a tradition worth relating here : The bell hanging in this church is associated with a deed of genuine Indian revenge. On its way from France it was captured by an English cruiser and taken to Salem, Massachusetts, where it was sold to the church at Deerfield, in the same state. The Indians, hearing of the destination of their bell, set out for Deerfield, attacked the town, killing forty seven of the inhabitants, and took 112 captives, among whom was the pastor and his family. The bell was then taken down and conveyed to St. Regis, where it now hangs.

During the next ten miles of our trip, the river is beautifully studded with islands, and resembles the

Thousand Islands scenery very much. Many of these islands are inhabited ; some of them elegantly laid out with drives, etc. Rev. Mr. Dickinson's, called after himself, has a dock at which steamers of this size can land ; it has a hotel, number of cottages, and is quite a gay place in summer. On the left side is Summers Town, beyond which is Hamilton's Island. Just before reaching Summers Town is the residence of Captain Cameron, formerly of this line ; beyond is the magnificent villa of Hon. Caribou Cameron, the finest on the St. Lawrence. It is built of Ohio freestone and cost $80,000. Hamilton Island, on the left, is occupied every summer by camping parties, who come from great distances, even from Virginia and Ohio, and remain two, three and even four months. Day after day, one of their principal amusements is rowing out in their small boats, awaiting the arrival of the steamers, and then swiftly riding on top of the swell that is occasioned by the wheels of the steamer. The scene is exciting and picturesque. On the right we now have a fine view of the Adirondack Mountains of Northern New York, and beyond the Green Mountains of Vermont, except it be a smoky or misty day, when the view is slightly obscured. It is fifty-six miles from the river to the mountains, and intervening is the wilderness of the State of New York, known as the John Brown tract, more famous as the hunting ground of adventurous hunting and fishing parties.

Continuing our course, we pass three small islands and enter Lake St. Francis, twenty-eight miles in length—a very picturesque sheet of water indeed ; but the trip through the lake is quite monotonous, therefore, for the next two hours, the guide, as well as the passengers, can "take a rest." This being a favorite route for honeymoon parties, there is now two full hours for these couples to enjoy the " honey " or the " moon," as seemeth to them best. After making this announcement one day, fifty-three left the deck ; one, however, was an old bachelor, who went to curl his hair.

In the center of the lake on the left, is the village of Lancaster, an old Scotch settlement. Just before reaching the village, is what appears to be a stack of hay, commonly known throughout Scotland as a Cairn. It is no more or less than a heap of stones in a rounded or conical form, placed in that way to commemorate some especial historic event. This one was built by the Glengarry Highlanders in 1847, to perpetuate the memory of Sir John Colburn, who was Commander in Chief of the Army and Governor-General of the provvince. It was built by putting cobble-stones one on top of the other—each individual inhabitant or stranger passing that way adding a stone. See Queen Victoria's Book, where she describes helping to build a Scotch Cairn with the assistance of John Brown, and one will get a better idea of how to build a Cairn. The county in which this place is located is named Glengarry, and is mainly or almost wholly inhabited by the sturdy Scotch Highlanders, whose farms are the finest in the Dominion. This is the last English speaking village on the route.

Passing three lighthouses, showing that the channel across the lake is quite intricate, we leave St. Anisette on the right, a small French town. We are now approaching the boundary line between the Provinces of Ontario and Quebec. The lighthouses on either side show the geographical divisions. From the lighthouse on the left the line runs straight to the Ottawa River; then the Ottawa becomes the dividing line. Just before arriving at the foot of the lake, where the river re-forms, we pass San Zotique; next Coteau Landing, where we call for the purpose of taking on a pilot,

EDWARD WILLETT,

whose duty it is to pilot this line of boats through the next series of rapids, and the Lachine, also through to Montreal; we are now coming to four rapids; first, the Coteau; second, Cedar; third, Split Rock, and fourth, the Cascades. The Canada Atlantic Railroad, running from Ottawa, the capital of the Dominion, to Coteau Landing, the railroad ferry at this point conveys whole trains to Valley Field, where connections are made for Boston and New York. A bridge was completed in 1890 and the ferry discontinued. The shortest route from the capital to those points. On the extreme right, at the foot of the lake, is the village of Valley Field. It is at the head of Beauharnois Canal, 11½ miles in length, which passes around this series of rapids. The river, in 11½ miles, has a fall of 84 feet. The finest water power privilege on the continent of America, except Niagara, is at this point. The largest cotton mill in the Dominion, the Canada Paper Co.'s mill, and several other manufacturing establishments are located at Valley Field. After leaving St. Francis Lake, we re-enter the river. With our pilot we go down the small rapid known as the Coteau, passing Prisoner's Island on the left, and on the left bank is the old French village of Coteau du Lac. On the extreme left, at the point, is an old French fort, where battles were fought in 1812 and 1813; the earthworks are still in a good state of preservation, behind which is the old saw-mill. Twenty minutes (or five miles) from this point to the Cedar Rapids, then you will "see der Rapid," that is a Rapid —the most Rapid Rapid of all the Rapids. Opposite the rapid is the village of Cedar on the left and St. Timothy on the right, the Cedar Rapid, the finest upon the St. Lawrence River. Look at St. Timothy, bear in mind the view you had of Morrisburg, the impression of its beauty and thrift, and now you have the comparison. How does the former strike you as against the latter? It is a historic fact, and worthy of note, that no matter what town you arrive at in the Province of Quebec, this will be apparent to the eye : the finest buildings in the place will be the church, nunnery, school, hospital, and the priest's residence. Aside from these, the rest are all about alike. You cannot tell the palace residence from the blacksmith's shop, or the grocery store from the hotel. The church at St. Timothy has a seating capacity of 1,500 ; the population of the village is 600 ; the church is always full on Sundays, and as Mark Twain exclaimed, " What large domes these worshippers must have to their pantaloons for 600 to fill a place capable of seating 1,500." But they come from all the country around, being all of one persuasion. An opposition church is so far unknown in these rural parts, hence it may be inferred what the extraordinary power of this old church must be in the lower province.

Speaking to one of the priests one day regarding the amount of money collected by them from the poor to build and maintain their institutions, I asked him how it was, and he remarked that the millions had more money than the millionaires, and by getting the dollar from the poorer classes they had the million, which the millionaires never give up.

Just before arriving at St. Timothy, we enter the Cedar Rapid and pass a distance of three and one-half miles in the extraordinary short time of seven minutes. By casting your eye shoreward, while passing an island on the left, and just before we enter the heaviest part of the rapid, you will discover how fast the boat is going. Looking to the right, you will see Hell's Hole and the greatest commotion in the river from Kingston to the Gulf.

Leaving Cedar Rapid, which is the most picturesque and beautiful (in our estimation) of all, two and one-half miles farther along, and passing Bockey Hayes' shoal, which is a peculiar formation in the bed of the river, making navigation somewhat dangerous. In illustration: One day the steamer "Corsican" suddenly lurched to the left, and evidently struck a rock ; whereupon the captain said to the pilot, " Edward, you are a little too far over to the left." Before he could complete the sentence the boat lurched to the right and struck another rock ; then the pilot replied, "Yes ; and a little too far over to the right side." It is plain that the channel about here is at least precarious. The government engineers, however, are now at work removing these dangerous obstructions. The Napoleon hats you see in the distance, on poles about ten feet high, are the marks which enable the pilot to obtain his true bearings through the shoal. Turning to the right, we come in sight of the Split Rock Rapid, the most dangerous rapid of all. When we speak of danger, we don't mean to life or limb, as no person was ever injured on this rapid ; it is danger to property that we refer to, as this is the only one of the series that has cost the company one dollar. They lost one steamboat here, and have had others upon the rocks. On the 8th of July, 1874, the steamer "Corinthian," of the R. O. N. Co., when passing the Split Rock Rapid, was almost instantly enveloped by a terrible thunder shower, accompanied by a hurricane. The wind was so powerful that the boat refused to answer the helm, and instead of turning to the right, as she should, the wind caused her to go straight ahead, and we struck a rock forward about five feet high and passed fifteen feet aft of the wheel over the same, and then stopped. I was upon the right-hand side of the boat explaining to the passengers and showing or pointing out to them the ledge of rock when she struck. Immediately four ladies caught hold of me (whom they thought was the boss life preserver). What a position for a nice young man. I was about to exclaim as my friend A. Ward did when he was surrounded by twenty of Brigham Young's wives, " I hope your intentions are honorable." However, through the assistance of some friends, I procured life preservers for them and was released from my somewhat precarious position. In the space of an hour most of the passengers were landed by the aid of the ship's boats and bateaux from the shore, and proceeded by rail to Montreal, where they arrived the same evening. I remained on board all night until a derrick was erected and two of the boats lashed together, and a platform built upon them, when I was let down by the aid of the derrick upon the same, and without further trouble taken to shore in safety. The second line of whitecaps which you see in the distance in front, is the Split Rock, a ledge of rock running from shore to shore, with the exception of a break of about sixty feet, which is a natural split in the rock.

Formerly there was only a depth of nine feet of water; it was blasted out and now gives a navigable channel of thirteen and one-half feet. Passengers, by looking into the water on the right side of the boat, can see the ledge we have been talking about.

One and a half miles from here to the Cascade, the last of this series of four, and the last but one on the river—the Lachine being the last. The Cascade differs from all the rest, being a cutting, chopping sea, in which the boats are wrenched more than in any other rapid. On the right is the village of Melocheville, at the foot of the Beauharnois Canal, eleven and one-half miles in length, that passes around this line of rapids. The boats of this and all other lines are compelled to pass through this canal, as none of them could ascend this line of rapids.

We are now thirty miles by water and twenty-four miles by land from Montreal. In the distance in front, is Mount Royal, or Montreal mountain. The park mountain drive, the most famous drive in the world, is up the brow of the mountain through a park. On the left is Il Perot Island, formed by the two channels of the Ottawa. The one we now see comes by St. Anne's, where Moore wrote his famous Canadian boat song. A resident of St. Anne's, Lieutenant-Colonel Dowker, says that every spring the freshets of the Ottawa cause the water to come down into the St. Lawrence with such force as to form an eddy to pass up the point of the island and down the navigable channel of the Ottawa, and he can take a pail from his house, Chateau Blance (where the famous poet Moore resided while at St. Anne's and wrote his Canadian poems) proceed down to the river and dip up a pail of pure, clear St.

Lawrence water. Meeting Colonel Dowker, he told me that the freshets of the Ottawa in March and April, 1885, were the most alarming and disastrous ever known. The sudden breaking up of the ice caused a jam. Houses were moved from their foundations, cattle and sheep crushed to jelly by the ice and many drowned ; the ice piled mountains high. The government had an agent in the vicinity relieving the distressed inhabitants. The heavy flow of ice by the freshets in the Ottawa caused a jam a little below Montreal in the year 1887, consequently flooding the city, causing much damage to life and property. The oldest church in the upper Province and old forts are to be seen here.

On the left a portion of the Ottawa empties into the St. Lawrence. This is not, however, the main channel ; the navigable portion of the river is just the other side of Il Perot. Note the difference between the color of the two waters ; they are as wide apart as green is from purple. The water of the Ottawa is of a dark brown color, caused by passing over low, marshy, peat bed soils, and the huge forests through which this river passes, the leaves falling and rotting, and swept along by the freshets, doubtless dye the water to the peculiar color observable. The waters of the two rivers do not readily mix, and each are distinct for many miles.

In the distance is Lake St. Louis, or Lachine Lake, 15 miles from the rapids to the foot of the lake, where we arrived at Lachine, on the left, and Caughnawaga on the right. The latter is the residence of the Indian pilot, St. Jean Baptiste, who discovered the channel and took this line of boats down the Lachine Rapids for over forty years.

About half way through the lake on the right we come to Nun's Island. That mound or elevation of ground which you see, was a fort in 1812, and English and American warlike parties met in sanguinary contest around here. It commands the entrance to the Chateaugay River. The village of Chateaugay is six miles back. The Nun's Island belongs to the Gray Nuns, of Montreal, who have a hospital for their own sick, and the spot is marked by a large cross, emblematic of their order.

Fifteen minutes from here we are in sight of Caughnawaga, where we formerly took on board the Indian pilot, who has become of historical interest to tourists, as it was he who discovered the channel and took the first of this line down, August 19, 1840, and has been in the employ of the company ever since. He is 75 years old, weighs 240 pounds, and stands six feet high. I am sorry to say that on account of age, the company were forced to retire him, and his brother-in-law will take the boats through the Lachine rapids this year. Many of the passengers imagine he is the only pilot who can take a boat through Lachine Rapids. This is not correct for we have other pilots who can ; but as he is paid for this especial service they resign most cheerfully in his favor. He has never had an accident and the company believe in holding to that which is good, and therefore, "stick to the old man." It was his custom to emerge from shore in a small boat accompanied by his two sons. They row him to the steamers; he comes on board and the boys go home again. He remains on board till the next morning, takes the first train for Lachine, where he is met by the boys, who take him home in a row boat. The Indian

WHEN YOU VISIT

SARATOGA,

STOP AT

THE ADELPHI

THE MOST COMFORTABLE AND HOME-LIKE
OF ALL SARATOGA HOTELS.

Location Perfect — Terms Moderate.

UNDER THE MANAGEMENT OF

Messrs. HAYES & BRUSHNIHAN.

The Sagamore,

On Green Island, Lake George.

ALL that is rich, striking and gorgeous in nature, beautified by art, to make the scene sublime and inspiring, has been done. :   :   :   :   :   :   :   :

Connected with the Main Land by Bridge.

ADDITIONS:

Two Queen Anne Cottages,
    Fifty Rooms for Guests,
        Magnificent Extra Dining Room,
            Music Hall and Ball Room.

This Splendid New Hotel is Open to Guests from

JUNE 20TH UNTIL OCTOBER 1ST.

IT IS SUPPLIED WITH

Passenger Elevator, Electric Lights and Bells in Every Room, as well as other Modern Conveniences. :   :   :   :   :

Its location the finest on the lake. The table is excellent, the service unsurpassed. Easy of access by Boats from the North or South, Baldwin or Caldwell, where trains with Palace Cars arrive from Saratoga, New York and intermediate points several times daily.

For Descriptive Circulars and Plan of Rooms, address

M. O. BROWN, Lessee and Proprietor,
    Bolton Landing, Warren Co., Lake George.

N. B.—The Finest Livery in the vicinity of Lake George.

FAMOUS FOR ONE-THIRD OF A CENTURY

THE
ST. LAWRENCE HALL,
MONTREAL.

It is so arranged that rooms used for guests are only, the balance of the GRAND NEW PARLORS, which are feet by feet at its widest is famed since. The item of roominess of the house is a matter of note and can be worthy of attention. The new Dining Room, Ladies Entrance, Grand Driving Room, Parlors and Suites of Rooms are added, the last furnished, furniture is the St. Lawrence.

The ST. LAWRENCE HALL, occupies a frontage of 250 feet on St. James 70 feet on St. Francois Xavier Streets, its principal entrance on St. George Street. It is in close proximity to the City Hall, Court House, the new Post Office. Thus

From $2 to $3 is Saved from HIGH Rate prices.

MURRAY HILL HOTEL,

Park Avenue, Fortieth and Forty-first Sts., New York
(One Block from the Grand Central Depot.)

A HOTEL OF SUPERIOR EXCELLENCE on both American and European plans. It occupies the highest ground in New York City, and is the *healthiest of locations*. For Transient Guests, Tourists, Travelers, or as residence for Families, none more cool, beautiful or pleasant can be found.

HUNTING & HAMMOND.

N. B.—Guests of the Murray Hill Hotel have their baggage transferred to and from the Grand Central Depot
FREE OF CHARGE.

UNITED STATES HOTEL
TOMPKINS, GAGE & CO., PROPRIETORS.
SARATOGA SPRINGS, N.Y.

FIRST-CLASS
In Every Respect.

OPEN

· FROM JUNE TO OCTOBER, ·

EACH YEAR.

TOMPKINS, GAGE & PERRY, - - Proprietors.

ST. LOUIS HOTEL

Quebec, Canada

THE LEADING HOTEL OF THE CITY

WM. O'NEIL, MANAGER

THE STEAMERS,

PURITAN, PILGRIM,
PLYMOUTH AND
PROVIDENCE,

OF THE

FALL RIVER LINE,

The Famous Business and Pleasure Route Between

NEW YORK AND BOSTON

Are the Four Leading Steamboats of the World, and are conceded to be the largest, handsomest and most perfectly equipped vessels of their class ever constructed. They steer by steam, are lighted throughout by electricity, and in every detail of equipment more than meet all possible conditions of the demands of first-class travel.

The Long Island Sound Route of the Fall River Line is one of the most attractive highways of travel to be found anywhere.

Tickets by this route are on sale at all the Principal Ticket Offices in the United States.

pilot's name is St. Jean Baptiste de Lisle; his Indian name, Ta ya ka, meaning in the U. S. language that "he will cross the river," but he does not; he goes down the rapids. He has a family of six children, three boys and three girls. The girls are unmarried. I state this for the benefit of the young men on board, as the Indian pilot says he wants a "heap Yankee" for his girls. I am engaged to my Mary Jane, and they can't have me.

A description of Caughnawaga would not be amiss. Note the line of palatial residences along the bank beyond the church, the windows and doors kicked out to give them light and air, the palace gardens in the front part of the back end of the house. The laundry of Caughnawaga is usually hung on the fence, it is not wash day to-day, as you can perceive. The bath-room is the whole water-front, but it is seldom used. The water-works is that barrel on the shore. The fair damsel waving her lily white hand is Mary Jane, my best girl. She comes out every day to welcome me, as she thinks I am on board. You can get her eye and have a flirtation, the same as I have had for years, and not make me jealous. That large brick structure is the centennial building, built during the centennial year by the celebrated Indian Chief, White Kicker. I think they used him to kick the windows and doors out of the palatial residences previously spoken of.

Caughnawaga, signifying "Praying Indian" (my friend Ben Butler says they spell it with an e), is well laid out for an Indian village with a population of 900, all Indians; no whites can live here.

The finest crops raised in this section of the country are raised just below Caughnawaga. They raise them with a derrick. It is a blasted crop, however, and of no use until it is. This notable quarry is where most of the stones come from for the construction of the locks in the new Lachine canal—the entrance to which is at Lachine, the village just passed at the foot of the lake, on the left.

THE VILLAGE OF LACHINE

is a favorite resort for Montrealers in summer. The inhabitants number about 2,000, but it is frequently augmented in the season to 9,000 or 10,000. Note the large buildings, which are the church, Villa de Marie Convent, the School and University for the education of priests.

Our pilot being on board, he will now show his Injin-uity in piloting a boat down the Lachine Rapids. Before reaching the rapids the tourists can see the aqueduct that supplies the city of Montreal with water.

THE LACHINE RAPIDS

differ from all the rest ; it is simply an intricate channel through rock. Take your position upon either side of the boat and you will know when we come to the most important point, as the boat will be headed direct for a little island which is nothing more or less than a few loads of dirt upon a huge ledge of rock. Keep your eye upon the bow of the boat and you will be led to exclaim, " why, we are going to strike the island ;" and if you are a betting person or a truthful one, you would almost swear we could not help but strike ; but when within less than ten feet, we make a very sudden turn to the right with a grand pitch or lurch, in which you will think the boat drops ten feet. We pass alongside of a ledge of rocks for about half a mile, to see which you must be upon the right hand side of the boat; at the end of this ledge of rock we have a perfect miniature Niagara, a little water-fall for a cent. Do not allow the lurching of the boat from side to side, to cause you any uneasiness, as there is no danger, because a side wheel boat has guards from four to ten feet projecting over on each side from the hull, 60 to 90 feet long, so that when that flat surface strikes the water by lurching, that is as far as she can go, therefore, will always righten herself immediately. I have had a great deal of sport in this way. When the boat had lurched over as far as she could, I would immediately exclaim: "Oh! I am on the wrong side," and proceed to the high side, when the boat would immediately righten up and the passengers would think I did it, but sh would have rightened without my aid. Yet I have heard some very strong-minded women, after seeing the effect of my moving to the high side of the boat, exclaim: " Put that big man off ; he has too much weight to be upon a boat in the rapids." This is the last rapid built on the St. Lawrence, you can have it the best one if you like and I will not quarrel with you for it. All I ask you to do is to stop at the hotels who advertise in my book and tell them I was the cause of your visit, and if they do not treat you well I will proceed to sit down upon them, not mentally, but physically, and they will never have occasion to treat any one else badly. Passing the foot of the rapids, a first view of Montreal on the left, and on the right is the village of La Prairie. The first mountain on the left is Mount Bruno ; second, Bellisle ; the third, St. Pie. The next and last sensation on the trip is passing under.

VICTORIA BRIDGE,

the largest and longest tubular bridge in the world, was built by Mr. Stephenson in 1860 for the Grand Trunk Railroad, by which it is owned and controlled. It is a mile and three-quarters of iron, two miles and a quarter with its approaches from shore. It is wholly of iron, top, bottom and sides—an iron tunnel or box, as it were. There are twenty-four abutments, built wedge-shaped (to crush the immense ice fields that pass through this section, which, previous to the building of the bridge, did immense damage to Montreal during the spring freshets. There are no such things as freshets on the St. Lawrence, the Ottawa flowing in some miles above causing such disasters), upon which rests the sections of iron. The spans are from 250 to 360 feet long each, and the center span is about 60 feet high. The bridge tubes are 16 x 22 feet. It contains no wagon road or foot path, and is used by the G. T. R. and its connecting lines. The cost of this immense work was $6,250,000, about one-half of which amount went to fatten the contractors. I was not one of them. I mention this on account of my size, and for fear some one might think I was wealthy. The bridge is constructed of sheets of iron with a two-inch edge turned up and riveted to each other. It is fastened to the center, loose on both ends on rollers, and is provided with a sliding track, so that there is no danger by expansion or contraction to passing trains. It expands and contracts from three and one-half to seven inches The bridge is kept in thorough repair and well painted. The small holes, or perforations in the sides of the bridge, were originally intended to convey the smoke out, but found inadequate for that purpose ; therefore they caused to be erected a line of flues the whole length. Now if any smoke remains it is carried out in a hand-basket. The two movable scaffolds you see are used by the workmen in repairing and painting.. It is not a draw bridge, and as we pass under the center span, and not over it, you need not remove your hat if you remain on the deck. After passing under the bridge you will have a magnificent view of

MONTREAL HARBOR.

The points of interest in the harbor will all be described to you as we pass over St. Lambert's shoal, a very dangerous passage, previous to landing at the Quebec boat, where we transfer such passengers as desire to visit Quebec. The island you see front on the right is St. Helen's Isle, used by the citizens of Montreal for pleasure, picnic parties, etc. A ferry plies between the city and the island every half hour, from morning until seven P. M. On Sunday from 3,000 to 20,000 persons visit the island, mostly French Canadains, three-fifths of whom comprise the population of Montreal. In the distant front on the left is the oldest church in Montreal; to the left of that, the largest building with the dome, is the Bonsecour Market and old City Hall. The new City Hall is that large building in the rear with the dome in the center and four columns—one in each corner. Across the road to the left, that long building, is the Court House. At the head of Jacques Cartier Square is a magnificent column erected to the memory of Admiral Lord Nelson. At the foot of the square lies a steamer of the Richelieu & Ontario Navigation Company.

There are two steamers on this line, notably the "Montreal" and "Quebec." The company owns twenty-one side-wheel boats. The Quebec line has the largest boats that float the St. Lawrence River; they will compare favorably with the boats of the Sound or the Hudson River—triple-decked palace boats, built of Bessemer steel; one has a capacity of 360 state rooms —the other 280. The distance to Quebec is 180 miles, and the fare on this line is only $2.50—the cheapest on the continent. Beyond, on the left, the two massive towers you see belong to the French church of Notre Dame. It is not a Cathedral, but simply a parish church. (The Cathedral is on Dominion Square, in process of erection, and when completed will be one-half the size of St. Peter's at Rome). It is the largest on the continent, and has contained within its walls, front porch and stairways, on the 24th of June (St. John's Day), twenty-two thousand souls. Beyond is the Custom House, with the clock in the tower, and still further up, the examining warehouse of the Custom House, as well as the office, docks and steamers of the Allen line. The first stop is at Quebec boat; passengers for Montreal remain on deck, as this line is compelled to enter the first lock of the Lachine canal; the gates close and the water is allowed to enter, which raises the boat to the level of the dock, when the passengers are allowed to depart. Montreal is the commercial metropolis of the Dominion, with a population of 160,000, three-fifths of which are French Canadians. The docks, piers, wharves, etc., of Montreal are the finest on the continent. It is the second city of commercial importance, New York being first. Six steamship companies leave here weekly for Europe during the summer season, and a large amount of business must of necessity be done, as its channel is closed during five months of the winter. The water front is all lighted with the electric light, so that work is carried on during the summer months night and day. On top of the revetment wall was built in 1889 a dyke or strong barricade ten feet high; it serves as a check to the water during the spring freshets to prevent the overflowing and damage of the sudden rise of previous years. Having selected your hotel and arrived at the same, our next duty will be to see the sights of

MONTREAL.

It is situated at the head of navigation for ocean vessels, 540 miles from the Gulf of St. Lawrence, on the Island of Montreal, which lies between the two great rivers of the North, the St. Lawrence and the Ottawa. The island is about 32 miles in length, and at its widest some ten in breadth; it is so fertile as to be called the Garden of the Province. The surface of the land is level, with the exception of the eminence of Mount Royal, which rises 550 feet above the river level. Mount Royal gives the name to the city which lies at its base. The settlement of the town was originally determined by the first explorer, Jacques Cartier, in 1535, at which time an Indian village, Hochelaga, occupied the spot. The permanent founding of the place, however, did not occur until 1642, and in one hundred years of growth thereafter it gathered a population of 4,000. It was under French rule until 1760, when it passed into the hands of the British. In 1832 the cholera raged in Montreal with great violence, carrying off 1,843 inhabitants in a population of about 30,000. In April, 1849, a political mob burnt the Parliament buildings, which were erected on McGill street, and the seat of Government was, in consequence, transferred to Quebec, thence to Toronto, and finally to Ottawa, where it remains. In July, 1852, a destructive fire laid waste a large portion of the city, burning 110 houses, and consuming property valued at $1,400,000. Notwithstanding these reverses, the city recovered, and to-day numbers a population of 160,000. Years of industry and enterprise have produced growth, and improvement in Montreal, such as but few American cities can boast of, and perhaps one—Chicago —has exceeded. At the beginning of the present century vessels of more than 300 tons could not ascend to Montreal, and its foreign trade was carried on by brigs and barges. Now ocean steamships of over 6,000 tons, the floating palaces of the Richelieu & Ontario Navigation Company, and ships from 700 to 6,000 tons from all parts of the world, occupy the wharves of the harbor, which are not equaled on this continent in point of substantial construction, convenience and cleanliness. The old part of Montreal, near the river, has narrow, incommodious streets ; but the new growth of the city toward Mount Royal has been liberally laid out, with wide and cheerful thoroughfares. The architecture here is very fine ; the material chiefly used is a zinc colored limestone, extensively quarried three miles from the city. The public buildings, banks and principal warehouses are solid and handsome enough to adorn a European capital. The great wealth of the Roman Catholic Church has enabled it to erect many magnificent churches, hospitals and convents, always in a very massive and enduring style. Other denominations seem to have been excited by emulation, and vie with each other in the beauty and elegance of their places of worship. Among the evidences of the French origin of the city are to be noticed a few curious old buildings to be found lingering here and there about Jacques Cartier Square, or occupying sites on the eastern part of the river front. The old houses are built somewhat like fortifications, and have heavy vaulted cellars, wherein treasure might be stored or a defense made against hostile foes, in the days when Indians and whites, French and British were fighting and plundering each other. The French Canadians in the city continue still to be a little more than half the population, and, although their language here has not been unaffected by the constant intercourse with English-speaking people, it is not, as commonly supposed, a *patois*, but such French as was spoken by the polite and educated in France, when the emigrants who first settled Canada left the shore of their mother-land. The naming of many of the streets of Montreal after saints and holy things, reminds one that its founders were not exiles nor adventurers, but enthusiastic missionaries.

PLACES OF INTEREST.

The Post Office is built on St. James Street, the chief thoroughfare of this city, opposite the New St. Lawrence Hall. The reason why I use the word new may be asked. Well, the hotel has been newly refitted, the corner building purchased, one hundred elegant and commodious rooms added, with baths and closets, electric bells and elevators, ladies' reception room, new and elegantly furnished suites of rooms added. The old proprietor, Mr. Hogan, pronounced by connoisseurs to be the best landlord in the dominion, has assumed the proprietorship and has associated with him as manager, Mr. Samuel Montgomery, the best choice that could be made, as he is an American from the Pacific slope, where they know how to keep a hotel. I therefore cheerfully recommend you to stop at the new St. Lawrence Hall during your stay in Montreal. Starting from there, it being the center, every point of interest is within fifteen minutes' walk of this hotel. The first building to the left is the new Post Office, recently finished, with a richly decorated exterior, and every internal improvement which modern ingenuity has devised. Opposite on the right is the celebrated Ed. McEntyre, The Merchant Tailor of Montreal, 116 St. James St. This location has beeh a merchant tailoring store for nearly a century. Mr. McEntyre has made my clothes for the past 18 years ; if he can fit me, further comments are unnecessary. Tell him I recommended you, he will treat you better for it. Adjoining is the Bank of Montreal, in the Corinthian style of architecture, with a sculpture on the pediment depicting native Indians, a sailor and settler with the emblems of the arts and trade. The corporation occupying this noble building is the richest one of the kind in America. It has branches in every town of importance in the Dominion, and has offices in New York, Chicago and London. It issues letters of credit on all parts of the world. Its capital and reserve fund amount to $18,000,000. Adjoining it is the Imperial Fire Insurance Co.'s new building. Crossing the street on the left hand corner, is the commercial building of the New York Life Insurance Company. Adjoining are other banks, having their offices on Place d'Arms,—the Jacques Cartier, Ontario, Quebec and National Banks.

On the south side of the square, the great parish church of Notre Dame looms up. The dimensions of this vast Norman edifice is 225 feet in length and 134 in width. Its towers are 230 feet high ; the western one contains the largest bell in America, "Gross Bourdon," in weight 29,400 pounds. The seating capacity of the church is 10,000. It has recently been decorated in deep colors and gold, after the manner of the St. Chappelle at Paris. An elevator was added making the tower easy of access to visitors. Suspended over the western gallery, and near the grand altar, is an immense wooden crucifix. This was brought from France two centuries ago, and first set up in the church built on the ground now Place d'Arms. Adjoining Notre Dame is the venerable Seminary of St. Sulpice, with its old gateway, courtyard and clock. The gentlemen of this seminary originally held valuable rights affecting the entire island of Montreal ; much of the land yet remains in their hands. With the wealth thus brought to their coffers, they have liberally established and conducted many institutions of charity and education scattered throughout the city. We are now on Notre Dame street, formerly the chief retail street in Montreal. Let us go on, we shall soon arrive at the Court House, a fine Grecian building of simple and massive appearance. A few steps further on the right brings us to Nelson's monument, setting forth in bas-relief the various victories which the great naval hero won without the loss of a single British ship. This monument is in Jacques Cartier Square, at the foot of which is the wharf of Quebec steamers.

Keeping on Notre Dame Street, directly beside the monument, we find opposite to each other two buildings which form a sharp contrast. The one on the left is the new City Hall, a lofty and ornate specimen of French architecture ; facing it is the " old chateau," a structure probably thought very fine a century ago, when Benjamin Franklin set up in it the first printing press ever used in the city. Now the old place is a Normal school, and the discoveries of the illustrious American are explained there, and let us hope his witty sayings repeated and acted upon. We can now take our way to the river side, and a block from Jacques Cartier Square shall find Bonsecours Market, a vast substantial Doric structure. Here, if it be market day, we may see a little of the French Canadian peasantry, clad in their homespun, and bargaining about their fowls, or eggs or butter, with many queer words and phrases now almost forgotten in the Normandy, whence they were first brought. Next to the market is Bonsecours Church, a rough-cast building with a high pitched roof, and with a breadth of a few feet adjoining it, occupied by cobblers and cake shops. This church is the oldest Roman Catholic one in the city ; its entrance is at the farthest side ; rarely is unoccupied by some worshippers from the adjacent market, who bring in, without ceremony, their baskets and bundles. Suspended over the altar is a model of a ship in bright tin, in which usually burning tapers are placed. Returning, on the water front, we note the ships and steamers from Liverpool, Glasgow, London, Havre, Rotterdam and other ports ; and on the right successively pass the Custom House, a triangular building, with a clock tower ; the office of the Allen line, also having a clock, and the fine building of the Harbor Commissioners. Next to it is a curious looking pile, with external hoistways from top to bottom ; this is the Customs Examining Warehouse. Before we leave this vicinity, we shall glance backward at the street from Allen's office to the Custom House.

Taking a short journey, still upon the river front, we come to the great works of stone-masonry, which give to Montreal an enlarged canal to Lachine, so that vessels of much greater tonnage than the ones at present used may be employed in the grain trade. This enterprise is one of a series of canal improvements by which Canada strives to retain and increase its business as a highway for the shipment of western produce to the sea-board.

Retracing our steps, we take the wide street running up from the river, McGill, and mark the fine warehouses that adorn it. Arriving at Notre Dame street, a little above, on the left, John Murphy & Co., branch houses in Glasgow, London and Ottawa. They buy for cash and sell for cash, one price marked in plain figures on all goods—which are the most reliable, who invite you to inspect their stock, styles and prices. Adjoining is Mr. S. Carsley, who occupies the six or seven stores in succession. Something should be said here relative to Mr. Carsley's establishment, which is admitted to be the finest as well as the largest in Canada. In doing so I shall not speak of the man but of the sterling features adopted as a guide in the past, which gave him prosperity and success. To secure the finest and best goods, fresh from the factories or trade centers, this establishment has its principal house in London, Eng., as well as a resident buyer there. It also selects four of the best judges of goods required for the home market, who go to the trade centers of Europe two or three times each year with "carte blanche" to make any purchases required. The imported as well as the domestic goods are all marked in plain figures, so that each purchaser may know the price; therefore a child can buy as well as a grown person. I cheerfully request you to visit this model establishment and inspect the styles, goods and prices, and if you do not make a purchase it will be because you will receive so much for your money that you will be afraid you cannot carry it home. Retracing our steps back to McGill street, we turn to the right, and immediately in front, just one block, is Victoria Square, which contains a statue of the Queen, by Marshall Wood. Corner St. James street, opposite, on the left, is the Albert Building. Turning to the right we enter St. James street. The first building of note on the right is the Ottawa Building; on the left is J. J. Milloy, the tailor, where tailor-made suits for ladies are a specialty. A little further on the right is G. W. Clark, the Universal Souvenir Palace, where, if you enter, the sight of such rare curiosities and splendid souvenirs will cause you to wonder how you got in without a ticket; and a little above is Drysdale & Co., where cheap English reprints of all the popular American authors may be had. This is the largest book store in Canada. Opposite on the left is R. Sharpley & Sons, No. 225, their new store; you are cordially invited to see and inspect their new stock. "Alexander's" is a little above, where is kept a first-class restaurant, confections, "bon-bons," etc., and you can be served with the best the market affords. On our way to the Post Office, from whence we started, at the corner of St. Peter street is the Mechanic's Institute. This building contains a good library, the admission fee to which is only nominal, and a very good reading room, having on its tables the principal dailies of America, the London *Times*, the Glasgow *Herald*, the Dublin *Warder*, the Edinburgh *Scotsman*, and all the weeklies, monthlies and quarterlies of both England and the United States. Strangers can have free access to this reading-room, for the period of two weeks, by applying to Mr. Hogan, the proprietor of the new St. Lawrence Hall. Opposite to the Mechanic's Institute is the Merchants Bank, built in modern Italian style, with polished granite columns at the entrance ; the interior of this bank should be seen ; the main office is carried up two stories in height and is beautifully frescoed. Diagonally across the street is Moulson's Bank, also of Italian design and richly decorated. We are now nearly at the hotel again, where we may conclude for the present our inspection of the city.

Resuming our sight-seeing, we shall now leave behind us the business streets, and take our way to the upper part of Montreal. Our suggestion is, to take St. James street to the first crossing on the right as you leave the hotel, St. Peter street. After two blocks this street changes its name to Bleury street. At No. 17 Bleury street, we may enter Notman's studio, a large handsome building entirely devoted to photographic art. Here we may spend half an hour very pleasantly in looking over views of Canadian scenery, and portraits taken singly or skillfully grouped, representing the sports and pastimes of our winter. The chief of these pictures is that which shows a carnival held at the Victoria Skating Rink eighteen years ago, when H. R. H. Prince Arthur was present. This distinguished representative of Royalty was stationed in Canada when quite a youth for two or three years—during his absence has won the title of Duke, married a Princess and during the early part of June 1890, paid Montreal a visit where he was right royally received. Mr. Notman photographed the Duke and Duchess in several styles of his art, and remarked to me that the interview was the pleasure of his lifetime. The photographic marvel spoken of above, with others now surrounding it on the walls of Mr. Notman, attracted great attention and admiration at the Centennial Exhibition. Mr. Notman was photographer to the exhibition, and received its highest awards.

Continuing on Bleury street, we soon reach, on the left, the Church of the Jesu, with St. Mary's College adjoining it, conducted by the Jusuit Fathers. This church is modeled after one of the same name at Rome, where the remains of Loyola are entombed. The style of architecture is the round Roman arch. The interior is one of the most beautiful among American churches. Over the high altar is a fresco of the crucifixion. In the southern transcept the sufferings of the first Canadian martyr, burnt by savages are depicted. Leaving the elegant house of prayer, we shall continue on Bleury street until we come to St. Catharine Street. A few steps bring us to the Nazareth Asylum for the Blind, attached to which (No. 1091) is a most ornate chapel, decorated in such a lovely manner as to lead one to suppose that it was done to encourage the suffering inmates of the asylum to see.

Next building on this side of the street (No. 1097) is the Roman Catholic Commercial Academy, a lordly monument of wealth and munificence, containing all the modern appliances for the practical training of youth, and presided over by an able staff of professors. If we keep going eastward on St. Catherine street, we pass on St. Dennis street the immense parish church of St. James, with the tallest spire in the city. Near by is the new church which is dedicated to Notre Dame De Lourdes ; water and relics from her shrine at Lourdes, in France, are for sale in the basement. Adjoining the church are its conventual buildings.

Returning on St. Catherine street, we soon come to Christ Church Cathedral (Church of England), unquestionably the most beautiful specimen of Gothic archi-, tecture in Canada. It is of a cruciform design ; its extreme width is 100 feet. The spire, which is entirely of stone, rises to the height of 224 feet. The materials of construction are Montreal limestone and stone from Caen in Normandy, which latter, by exposure to the weather, has changed from almost pure whiteness to a yellow tint. On the grounds of the Cathedral are erected the residences of the bishop and his assistants, the Synod Hall, and also a fine monument to Bishop Fulford, the first Metropolitan of Canada. The street running on the farther side of the Cathedral is University Street, and No. 82, one block distant, is the Natural History Museum, containing a good Canadian collection. University street leads us down to Dorchester street, on the corner of which is the St. James Club House. On the opposite corner is the Free Fraser Library Building. Taking Dorchester street eastward, we pass on the left St. Paul's Church (Presbyterian). On the same side we soon have a view of the vast proportions of the new St. Peter's Roman Catholic Cathedral.

Across the square on which St. Peter's is building, we notice a beautiful church, St. George's (Church of England), and adjoining it is the Sunday School, the largest and best conducted in Canada. On Dorchester street, fronting Dominion Square on Peel street, is the Windsor Hotel. A little below on Windsor street is the new depot of the Canada Pacific R. R., the largest and grandest in Canada. Next beyond on Dorchester street is the Victoria Skating Rink, where immense carnivals are held in the winter—the grandest in the world. In the summer the spacious edifice is used for concerts, walking matches, public gatherings, meetings, etc.

Two blocks distant is the foundling hospital of the Gray Nun, a visit to which is thus described : " A long procession of the nuns marched slowly into the chapel and knelt in prayer. Each nun had a crucifix and a string of beads attached, and whatever may have been the case with their thoughts, their eyes never wandered, notwithstanding strangers were gazing at them. Some were young and pretty, others old and plain, but the sacred character of their labor of love invested them all with beauty. We said the eyes of none wandered. Perhaps we ought to confess that the quick, sharp glance of one, apparently younger than the others, stared at us for a moment ; but it was only curiosity—womanly curiosity—and what woman has not the curiosity to look at me? Yet that moment was fruitful of thought, and as we saw the sad, dark-eyed beauty rise in her place and mechanically follow her more staid sisters, our mind went back to the days of chivalry, when gallant knights rode with lance at rest, or wielded the heavy battle axe in heroic deeds that they might win recognition from the proud ladies who looked down upon them. And as we thought, it seemed that the most gallant deeds that men of this nineteenth century might do, would be to rescue young and pretty nuns—who wanted to be rescued, from the silence and sadness of the nunnery." Again, on our way, we are arrested by an immense structure even larger than the institution just passed ; it is the Montreal College, which educates ecclesiastics, and also day pupils, and is under the care of the Sulpician fathers. Two Martello towers in front of the college are relics of the times when incessant strife raged between the settlers and the Indians. Sherbrooke street is adorned with the private residences of which the citizens of Montreal are proud, and in your drive around the town, previous to or after returning from Park Mountain drive, it will repay one to drive through Sherbrooke, Dennis and Dorchester streets. The McGill College, University and spacious grounds are the next points.

As we pass along Sherbrook street, in the distance we observe as we glance up St. Famille street, the enormous Hotel Dieu, with a large, bright dome, a free hospital for all, under Roman Catholic direction.

Returning to the postoffice, preferably by Beaver Hall Hill, we shall not fail to be struck by the number of handsome churches erected there together. On the right is the Unitarian Church ; on the left, successively, a Presbyterian, Baptist and a Jewish Synagogue. Near by, on Craig street, is a towered building occupied by the Young Men's Christian Association.

We are soon at the new St. Lawrence Hall, and before mentioning the drive that may be taken outside the city, it may be well to call attention to a few places near at hand a business man or student may be interested in visiting : The Corn Exchange, foot of St. John street ; the Merchant's Exchange, St. Sacrament street ; the office of the Telegraph Co., and the Open Stock Exchange, St. Francis Xavier street. Near the beginning of St. James street, on St. Gabriel street, is the Geological Museum, open daily from 10 to 4, containing an admirable collection of North American minerals, and many interesting fossils. Here may be seen what many geologists regard as the most primitive record of life, the *Eozoon Canadense*, first noticed at Perth, Ontario, by a Mr. Wilson. From the fact that the oldest fossil bearing stratum, the Laurentian, is the backbone, geographically, of Canada, and because of the great variety of rocks found in the immediate vicinity of Montreal, this museum is particularly attractive to a lover of science. An effort is on foot to deprive the city of this collection, and for the sake of centralization, remove it to Ottawa. I offer this as an apology in case it should be removed.

DRIVES.

As I have said two or three times, by far the most pleasant drive is up the brow of Mount Royal, called the Park Mountain Drive. There are presumably, two roads; the shorter returns by McTavish street, the other by Bleury. The park was laid out by Mr. Olmstead, the designer of Central Park, New York, whose achievements there were recognized by a statue adorning one of the entrances. The river view from Mount Royal is delightful, and must be seen to be appreciated. I dare not attempt to describe it. A suggestion of how to get a hundred pictures of every conceivable shape or form of landscape views, containing mountain, plain, river, lake, hillside, valley, etc., etc., is to close the eyes, place the hands on each end of the forehead, and every time the carriage moves a hundred feet open the eyes, and you have an entire new picture. Keep this up until you have had an elegant sufficiency of view. The next drive is around the mountain, and was the best until the completion of the Park mountain drive ; it is pleasant and attractive, when it includes a drive to the Catholic and Protestant cemeteries, giving a view of the monuments and tombs. The drive to Lachine is next, and is of interest. The drive to Longue Point, along the St. Lawrence in the opposite direction to the last, gives us an entirely different kind of scenery. It takes us through the village of Hochelaga, the terminus of the new railroad, the Quebec, Montreal, Ottawa & Occidental, which runs along the north shore of the St. Lawrence, and develops tracts of country as yet unbenefited by the iron horse. About a mile from the depot is the beautiful convent of the Sisters of the Holy names of Jesus and Mary. Many young ladies from the United States have been educated at this convent. The next noteworthy building is the Lunatic Asylum. This immense house, containing nearly 300 maniacs, idiots and imbeciles, is controlled by the Sisters of Providence ; these ladies, with the exception of six guardians for desperate characters, and a physician, have sole charge. They find no trouble in the care of the numerous inmates, and by their kindness and tact restore mental balance, in all the cases where cure is possible, in a tithe the time it used to take in the old days, when the insane were treated with harshness and cruelty. On our way to Longue Point, the village of Longueuil, Boucherville and Varennes lie on the opposite bank of the river. The drive to the Back River is an attractive one, and with citizens the most attractive of all ; the beautiful convent of the Sacred Heart is situated here, and its grounds, finely laid out, lead directly to the water's edge. The bridge which spans the river at this place—a branch of the Ottawa—affords one of the characteristic sights of Canada, the piloting of a raft through a tortuous channel. The size of an ordinary raft, its great value, from $100,000 to $300,000, the excitement of the captain and his French and Indian crew, with the constant perils threatening the whole structure, all conjoin to make up a scene to be dwelt upon and long remembered. Thus hoping the same will be said of your visit to Montreal, I shall advise you to visit

QUEBEC.

Tourists can either take the Grand Trunk, the North Shore or the Richelieu & Ontario Navigation Co.'s line of steamers. Tickets can be procured of the company's agent opposite the new St. Lawrence Hall building, where state rooms, etc., may be secured. I assume that the river is the route selected, and that the reader is fairly on his way to that ancient city and former capital. Passing a group of islands below Montreal and the mouth of the Ottawa River, we soon arrive at

SOREL,

forty-five miles below—the first landing made by the steamer. It was built upon the site of a fort built in 1755, by M. De Tracy, and was for many years the summer residence of many successive Governors of Canada. Five miles below, the broad expanse of the river is called

LAKE ST. PETER,

which is about nine miles wide. The St. Francis River enters here. Large rafts are observed here slowly floating to the great mart of Quebec.

THREE RIVERS

is situated at the confluence of the Rivers St. Maurice and St. Lawrence, ninety miles below Montreal, and the same distance above Quebec. It is one of the oldest settled towns in Canada, having been founded in 1618. It is well laid out and contains many good buildings, among which are the Court House, the Jail, the Roman Catholic Church, the Ursuline Convent, the English and Wesleyan Churches. The population of Three Rivers is about 9,200.

BASTICAN

is situated on the north shore of the river, one hundred and seventeen miles below Montreal. It is the last place the steamers stop at before reaching Quebec. It is a place of little importance.

In passing down the St. Lawrence from Montreal, the country upon its banks presents a sameness in its general scenery until we approach the vicinity of Quebec. The villages and hamlets are decidedly French in character, generally made up of small buildings, the better class of which are painted white or whitewashed with red roofs. Prominent in the distance appear the tile-covered spires of the Catholic churches, which are all constructed in that unique style of architecture so peculiar to that church.

During your stay in Quebec stop at the St. Louis Hotel, and if carriages are desired the hotel will furnish the same. Tourists are invited to visit the Fur Wareroom adjoining the Ladies' Parlor, containing one of the largest and most valuable stocks of furs in Canada at moderate prices. Ladies' sacques, caps and muffs, etc. There are four splendid drives laid out for the visitor and tourist ; a neat little pamphlet descriptive of the same, entitled " Views of the city of Quebec," will be given you by asking the clerk, Mr. W. G. O'Neill, Manager, or the news agent, of the St. Louis Hotel. They are instructed not to give them "*free*," unless you say I sent you for one or show them this notice.

CITY OF QUEBEC.

Quebec, by its historic fame and its unequaled scenery, is no ordinary or commonplace city, for though, like other large communities, it carries on trade, commerce and manufactures; cultivates art, science and literature ; abounds in charities, and professes special regard to the amenities of social life, it claims particular attention as being a strikingly unique old place, the stronghold of Canada, and, in fact, the Key of the Province. Viewed from any of its approaches, it impresses the stranger with the conviction of strength and permanency. The reader of American history, on entering its gates or wandering over its squares, ramparts and battle-fields puts himself at once in communion with the illustrious dead. The achievements of daring mariners, the labors of self-sacrificing Missionaries of the Cross, and the conflicts of military heroes, who bled and died in the assault and defence of its walls, are here re-read with ten-fold interest. Then the lover of nature in her grandest and most rugged, as in her gentler and most smiling forms, will find in and around it an affluence of sublime and beautiful objects. The man of science, too, may be equally gratified, for here the great forces of nature and secret alchemy may be studied with advantage. Quebec can never be a tame or insipid place, and with moderate opportunities for advancement, it must become one of the greatest cities of the New World in respect to learning art, commerce and manufactures.

The city of Quebec was founded by Samuel de Champlain in 1608. In 1622 the population was reduced to fifty souls.

In June, 1759, the English army under General Wolfe landed upon the Island of Orleans. On the 12th of September took place the celebrated battle of the Plains of Abraham, which resulted in the death of Wolfe and the defeat of the French army. A force of 5,000 English troops, under General Murray, were left to garrison the fort. The city is very interesting to a stranger ; it is the only walled city in North America.

Cape Diamond, upon which the citadel stands, is three hundred and forty-five feet in height, and derives its name from the quantity of crystal mixed with the granite below its surface. The fortress includes the whole space on the Cape.

Above the spot where General Montgomery was killed, is now the inclined plane, running to the top of the bank ; it is five hundred feet long, and is used by the Government to convey stores and other articles of great weight to the fortress.

THE CITADEL

will, perhaps, prove the point of greatest interest to many, from the historical association connected therewith, and from the fact that it is considered an impregnable fortress. It covers an enclosed area of forty acres, and is some three hundred and forty feet above the river level. The zigzag passages through which you enter the fortress, between high and massive granite walls, are swept at every turn by formidable batteries of heavy guns. On the forbidding river walls and at each angle of possible commanding point, guns of heavy calibre sweep every avenue of approach by the river. Ditches, breast works and frowning batteries command the approaches by land from the famed "Plains of Abraham." The precipitous bluffs, rising almost perpendicularly from the river three hundred and forty feet, present a natural barrier which may be swept with murderous fire, and the covered ways of approach and retreat, the various kinds and calibre of guns, mortars, howitzers, and munitions of war, will be viewed with eager interest. Among the places of note may be mentioned the Plains of Abraham, with its humble monument marking the place where fell the illustrious Wolfe ; the Governor's Garden, with its monument to Wolfe and Montcalm ; the spot where fell the American General, Montgomery ; St. John's Gate, the only gate remaining of the five that originally pierced the walls of the city ; the Roman Catholic Cathedral, with its many fine old paintings ; the Episcopal Cathedral ; the Esplanade, from which is one of the finest views in the world ; House of Parliament ; Spencer Wood, the residence of the Lieutenant Governor, Laval University, &c., &c.

The city and environs abound in drives, varying from five to thirty-five miles, in addition to being on the direct line of travel to the far-famed Saguenay, Murray Bay, Kamouraska, C-C.Seeacouna, Rimouski Gaspe, and other noted watering places.

Quebec can minister abundantly to the tastes of those who like to fish, yacht, or shoot. Yachting, in fact, has become of late the leading recreation in Quebec. You can on those mellow Saturday afternoons of August and September, meet the whole sporting and fashionable world of Upper Town on the Durham Terrace or Lower town wharves, bent on witnessing a trial of speed or seamanship between the " Mouette," the " Black Hawk," the " Wasp," the " Shannoh," the " Bonhomme Richard," and half a score of crack yachts, with their owners.

Let us see what the city contains :—First the west wing, built about 1789, by Governor Haldimand, to enlarge the old chateau burnt down in January, 1734 ; this mouldering pile, now used as the Normal School, is all that remains of the stately edifice of old, overhanging and facing the Cul-de-Sac, where the lordly Count de Frontenac held his quasi regal court in 1691 ; next, the Laval University, founded in 1854, conferring degrees under its royal charter ; the course of study is similar to that of the celebrated European University of Louvain ; then there is the Quebec Seminary, erected by Bishop Laval, at Montmorency, in 1663; the Ursuline Convent, founded in 1836 by Madame de la Peltrie ; this nunnery, with the Roman Catholic Cathedral, which was built in 1646, contains many valuable paintings, which left France about 1789 ; the General Hospital, founded two centuries ago by Monseigneur de St. Vallier ; in 1659, it was the chief hospital for the wounded and the dying of the memorable battle of the 13th September ; Arnold and his Continentals found protection against the rigors of a Canadian winter behind its walls in 1775-6 ; the Hotel

Dieu Nunnery, close to Palace Gate, dating more than 200 years back.

As to the views to be obtained from Durham Terrace, the Glacis and the Citadel, they are unique in grandeur. Each street has its own familiar vista of the surrounding country.

THE SHRINE AND FALLS OF STE. ANNE.

At the distance of about twenty miles below Quebec is the village of Ste. Anne de Beaupre, sometimes called Ste. Anne du Nord, and always called *La Bonne Ste. Anne*, to whom is consecrated the parish church, erected about four years ago by the Pope into a shrine of the first order, in which is a fine painting by the famous artist Le Brun, Ste. Anne and the Virgin, presented by M. de Tracey, Viceroy of New France, in 1666, to the church, for benefits received. The festival day of this Saint is the 26th of July, at which time thousands of pilgrims proceed not only by steamer and carriage, but on foot, to this holy shrine ; many walk the whole distance from Quebec to the church as a penance, or in performance of vows. The church is a new building, the old one having been found too small for the accommodation of the crowds of pilgrims who resorted there. In it are placed thousands of crutches, left by those who departed after being cured of the lameness and other maladies by the Bonne Ste. Anne, whose praises are world wide, for hither congregate daily thousands of pilgrims from all parts to be cured of their infirmities. Deposited in the sanctuary is a holy relic, being a finger bone of the saint herself, on kissing which the devotee is immediately relieved of all worldly ills and misfortunes. Wonder begins and misbelief vanishes on gazing at the piles of crutches; there one beholds unmistakable evidence of the unlimited medicinal powers of the mother of the Virgin. Daily are the proofs of this power; the stranger can see with his own eyes the decrepit, the halt, the sore, the lame, the wounded carried into the holy sanctuary and depart therefrom, after kissing the holy relic, cured and whole. Many are the scenes here witnessed of the despairing filled with renewed hope, and the feeble and faint glad again with strength and health. Countless are the anecdotes of the hopelessly blind and lame returning to their friends with sight and firm limbs, leaving behind them their bandages and crutches. Incredulity vanishes before such evidence, and the sceptic leaves the shrine of Ste. Anne with convictions deeply settled in his soul. Within three miles of the village are the Falls of Ste. Anne, which consist of seven cascades, one of which rushes through a narrow chasm, which can be leaped by one of strong nerves and sinews, but powerful as Ste. Anne is, and devoted as she is to miracles, it is doubtful whether even she could save the unfortunate who misses his leap.

The fishing above and below the Falls is very good for both salmon and trout, and the scenery of that wild description generally characteristic of the Laurentian ranges.

MONTMORENCY FALLS

are seven miles below Quebec. The road is very pleasant, passing through the French village of Beauport. Those who expect to see a second Niagara will be somewhat disappointed, as far as volume is concerned. The stream descends in silvery threads, over a precipice 265 feet in height, and, in connection with the surrounding scenery, is extremely picturesque and beautiful, but does not inspire the awe felt at Niagara. On June 8, 1887, with some friends we paid this delightful place a visit, and were entertained by the hotel proprietor, Mr. T. Bureau, in royal style, which, after the tramp over all the grounds and down the three hundred and sixty-five steps with the thermometer 85° in the shade, will always be retained as one of the grandest spots in memory.

POINT LEVIS,

on the other side of the river, opposite Quebec, will interest the stranger very much, immense and stupendous fortifications being in process of erection. Most tourists visiting Quebec pay the Saguenay a visit. The ticket office of this line is opposite the St. Louis Hotel, where my genial friend, Mr. R. M. Stocking, or his assistant, Mr. Henry Harris, will cheerfully impart any information required, he being the agent for all railroads and steamboats in Canada or that connect with the same in the United States.

TO SUMMER TOURISTS.

Visit St. Lawrence Hall Caconna. This elegant and spacious hotel, situated at the beauitful and fashionable Canadian Watering place on the Lower St. Lawrence, one hundred and twenty miles below Quebec, opposite the mouth of the far-famed Saguenay River, opened for guests June 15th, under the management of an

American of hotel fame, who for many years has been connected with the leading hotels in the United States. Mr. R. M. Stocking's ticket office opposite St. Louis Hotel will secure rooms for you at St. Lawrence Hall Caconna by telegraph without extra charge.

RIVER SAGUENAY.

To the pleasure-seeker or the man of science, there can be nothing more refreshing and delightful, nothing affording more food for reflection or scientific observation, than a trip to that most wonderful of rivers, the Saguenay. On the way thither, the scenery on the Lower St. Lawrence is extraordinarily picturesque ; a broad expanse of water, interspersed with rugged solitary islets, highly cultivated islands, and islands covered with trees to the water's edge, hemmed in by lofty and precipitous mountains on one side, and by a continuous street of houses, relieved by beautifully situated villages, the spires of whose tin covered churches glitter in the sunshine, affords a prospect so enchanting that were nothing else to be seen, the tourist would be well repaid ; but when, in addition to all this, the tourist, suddenly passes from a landscape unsurpassed for beauty into a region of primitive grandeur, where art has done nothing and nature everything ; when at a single bound, civilization is left behind and nature stares him in the face, in naked majesty ; when he sees Alps on Alps arise, when he floats over unfathomable depths. through a mountain gorge, the sublime entirely overwhelms the sense of sight and fascinates imagination.

The change produced upon the thinking part of man, in passing from the broad St. Lawrence into the seemingly narrow, and awful, deep Saguenay, whose waters leave the sides of the towering mountains which almost shut out the light of heaven, is such tha' no pen can paint or tongue describe. It is a river one should see if only to knc wh⋅⋅ dreadful aspects nature can assume in wild n⋅⋅⋅⋅⋅ Compared to it the Dead Sea is blooming, and t⋅ ⋅ ⋅⋅⋅st ravines cosy and smiling ; it is wild and grand, appare ⋅⋅ly in spite of itself. On either side rise cliffs varying in perpendicular height from 1,200 to 1,600 feet, and this is the character of the River Saguenay from its mouth to its source. Ha! Ha! Bay, which is 60 miles from its mouth, affords the first landing and anchorage. The name of this bay is said to arise from the circumstances of early navigators proceeding in sailing vessels up a river of this kind for 60 miles, with eternal sameness of feature,. stern and high rocks on which they could not land, and no bottom for their anchors, at last broke out into a laughing Ha! Ha! when they found landing and anchorage.

This wonderful river seems one huge mountain rent asunder at some remote age by some great convulsion of nature. The reader who goes to see it (and all ought to do so who can, for it is one of the great natural wonders of the continent,) can add to the poetical filling up of the picture from his own imagination.

This beautiful trip is easy and facile of accomplishment as new and magnificent boats, rivaling in luxuriousness with any in our inland waters, run regularly to Ha! Ha! Bay, on board of which the pleasure seeker will experience all that comfort and accomodation which is necessary to the full enjoyment of such a trip.

To the foregoing descriptions we append an extract from the letter of a writer in the Buffalo *Commercial*

Advertiser, who has apparently gone over the "ground" with much satisfaction. Speaking of the great pleasure route he says :

"There is probably no route in the known world presenting more attractions to the tourist than that from Buffalo to Montreal and Quebec, via Lake Ontario and the St. Lawrence River ; presenting, first, the visit to the great Cataract, next, Lake Ontario, the River St. Lawrence, and the romantic scenery of the 'Thousand Isles ;' then the sublime rapids, increasing in grandeur, to the great culmination of the 'Lachine Rapids,' and finally finishing with the beautiful scenery of and around the falls of Montmorency, at Quebec, and down the Saguenay—all combine to make up more of the wild, romantic and sublime than can be found in the same number of miles and almost any traveled route in the known world."

Returning to Montreal for our trip down Lake Champlain and Lake George, to Saratoga, Albany, New York and Boston, as most of the tourists have tickets to these destinations, the routes need only be mentioned. The Delaware & Hudson Canal Company Railroad, and Central Vermont have ticket offices in Montreal, where information is courteously dispensed by obliging, gentlemanly clerks at all times. It would be useless here to print the time tables of the different roads, as changes occur too often for such information to be reliable. As you are supposed to be quartered at the new St. Lawrence Hall, which is in the heart of the city, and contains the Grand Trunk Railroad and Delaware & Hudson Canal Company offices, where at all times may be found Mr. W. H. Henry, the Delaware & Hudson Company's genial Agent for the Dominion of Canada, directly opposite is the Central Vermont office, presided over by A. C. Stonegrave, any time-table required is easily obtainable ; a little above on right hand corner is the Richelieu and Ontario Navigation Company.

BURLINGTON, VT.,

is a beautiful city on the shore of Lake Champlain, and has many points of interest to see well worth visiting. The Van Ness is the leading hotel and has just been newly fitted up, and is a thoroughly equipped and well managed house. Such is Burlington.

Come and see for yourself.

BLUFF POINT,

one hundred and sixty-four miles from Albany, a'nd fifty-three miles from Montreal, is the most sightly point on Lake Champlain. The new and elegant Hotel Champlain, with its spacious grounds, unrivaled views and superb appointments, is situated on this commanding promontory. The bluff is about two hundred feet above the lake, and the view from the hotel includes about fifty miles of the lake and the Green and Adirondack Mountain Ranges. There are 363 acres in the hotel grounds, mostly wooded, which have been laid out in walks and drives. The hotel is 400 feet long, having an average width of about fifty feet, and a central width of about ninety feet. This immense and costly structure is surmounted by three towers, one at each end, and a central tower 125 feet high.

It is intended that the "Champlain" shall be the model summer hotel of its kind. The house and its furnishings are of the highest class, and every convenience that can conduce to the pleasure and comfort of its guests has been provided. Such has been the rapid growth in popularity of Lake Champlain that the opening of this fine home for summer pleasure seekers signalizes an era of interest in this incomparable region that has placed its shores in the front rank of summer resorts. Trains on D. & H. Co. R. R. leave Montreal every morning and afternoon, when passengers, who have tickets by that line can stop over at Bluff Point Station, and visit the grandest and best of all the Northern Adirondack Hotels, just opened this season, Hotel Champlain, and resume their journey when desired.

Leaving Montreal in the morning, by taking the first train on the Delaware & Hudson Canal Railroad, if you wish to make Hotel Champlain, Lake George, Saratoga or Albany the same day, your tickets my read Lake Champlain Co. Steamers, but it is all the same—boat and rail belong to the same parties. Should you desire to take Lake Champlain, leave Montreal in the afternoon and go to Bluff Point or Au Sable Chasm, via Port Kent, remain over night at Lake View House, taking the boat at 8 A. M., from there to Fort Ticonderoga, and then down Lake George, or proceed on the train in the morning or by boat. By getting off at Port Kent, changing cars to the Keesville, Au Sable Chasm & Lake Champlain Railroad, you will soon arrive at Au Sable Chasm Station. The busses in waiting will convey you to the Lake View House, where "mine host," W. H. Tracey, will see that all your wants and desires are satisfied. I had the pleasure of passing over the above railroad in June last, and must confess it quite a novel ride, with very picturesque scenery. I am the heaviest

Director of this road, weigh three hundred and thirty pounds—direct hundreds of passengers every year to pass over it. Hope the General Passenger Agent, A W. Boynton, will note this, so I will not be obliged count the ties next September when I return to visit A ɩ Sable Chasm. Therefore, it may be said if you desire to make both lakes on the same day, you are compelled to leave Montreal in the afternoon, and go to Au Sable Chasm via Port Kent, and remain over night at the Lake View Hotel, which will be found to be an excellent house, taking the boat in the morning. If tickets read by the Central Vermont Railway, you go to Burlington, where you arrive for supper, and as the boat does not leave until nine o'clock in the morning, you have plenty of time to see that beautiful city before the leaving of the boat ; at any rate you won't have to rise as early as you would if you were at Plattsburg.

MY FIRST VISIT TO AU SABLE CHASM.

As long as anything shall remain green in my memory, I feel confident it will be the impression of that charming view and grand natural spectacle, Au Sable Chasm.

Arising early in the morning if not with the lark, a very good second in the race, I was invited by the manager of the Lake View House to visit the chasm. Accepting the same, we proceeded through the gate and down the steps which I did not stop to count ; but the number was sufficient for a man of my weight, and as large bodies move slowly, I was behind the rest of our gay, hilarious party, because I remained to drink in the beauties my eyes were feasting upon. Reaching the end of the chasm, where we take the boat for the rapids, I did not have confidence to proceed the rest of the journey with my companions (as I felt I was too large a crowd for the boat), but, returning, as I came, which very few people do, I was more impressed by the grandeur of the scenery—more than going down. Returning to the hotel some hours after my party, I had stories to tell that caused many of them to return and make the trip that I had. If there is any view on earth that will please you it is the one obtained from any point at the lake view House, Au Sable Chasm, looking at Lake Champlain and the Green Mountains of Vermont on one side, and the Chasm or Adirondacks on the other.

Before the completion of the railroad, boats left Rouse's Point, on Lake Champlain, and a train left Montreal to connect ; but as the route on Lake Champlain has been discontinued from Rouse's Point to Plattsburg, really the most picturesque part of the trip down Lake Champlain being cut off, most of the tourists take the rail in the morning from Montreal and can pass through Lake Champlain by rail, or stop over, if but a short time, at Bluff Point station on D. & H. Co. R. R., and visit the grand "Hotel Champlain" where all the steamers on the lake land and receive passengers every regular trip. The rail passing close along the lake shore, one gets a very nice view, better, as I have often expressed it, than if the parties were on the boat, as they cannot see both shores on a boat at once, unles the tourist's eyes were cut out on a bias or cross, thus enabling them to see both sides at once. The rail is preferable and saves time. As it is immaterial to me how you reach Ticonderoga, it is presumed you get there. Lake George Junction is where you change cars, and connect for Baldwin, which is a ride of about fifteen minutes. You are now supposed to have arrived on board the company's steamers, "Horicon" or "Ticonderoga," and are sailing up Lake George. Now, if the reader expects me to describe Lake St. George, I shall simply say No ! with a large N. It is too much ; its praises have been written and sung for the past half century by thousands. I shall with pleasure and relief to myself, ask the loan of your scissors. Thanks ; now we can comply with your wishes : We have started on our trip through the magical lake. It is difficult to describe the quiet delight one feels as he gazes on the expanse of the tranquil azure spread before him like a part of the sky inlaid on the emerald bosom of the earth. Peace is in the very air which lazily slumbers over the water, while the monotone of the silvery ripples rolling over the yellow sands, and the musical moan of the breeze in the cone-cented pines, seem to carry the soul back to other days. Lake George is, indeed, like a work of art of the highest order, for it has the quality of improving, the more one studies its attractions, and the ever harmonious flow of lines constantly suggests a composition of consummate genius in which every effect has been combined to produce a certain ideal.

Now, dear reader, I have a favor to ask of you ; read this little book as far as Saratoga description commences ; then lay it aside and feast the eyes on Lake George for the next two hours, and, if you can describe its beauties, do so to the best of your ability, and forward to me, 21 Chestnut Park, Rochester, N. Y., and it shall have a place in this work, and you shall have the credit for the same ;—the task was too much for me.

CAMPING OUT.

The lake is a famous camping ground, during July and August, and its enjoyments, with bits of sound advice, cannot be better given than by the following, unless you purchase one of the favorite Guides to Lake George, Lake Champlain and the Adirondacks—full of information, maps and illustrations, published at Glen Falls, N. Y., and for sale on all steamers and news stands.

"The lovely islands are suddenly astir with busy throngs. Rocks are decked with blue and gray, the tree-tops blush with buntings ; shores put on a flannelly hue, and shadowy points blossom out in duck and dimity. It is safe to say that in the course of the season a thousand people taste the pleasures and overcome the difficulties that but season the glorious dish of camp life at Lake George. Among the necessaries are a light axe, long handle frying-pan, tin pail for water or coffee, tin plate, tin cup, knife and fork, and fishing tackle. A stove top laid on a fire-place of stones and mud, and supplied with one length of stove-pipe, is a positive luxury to the cook. Spruce boughs for a bed, with two or three good woolen blankets for covering, will be found very comfortable ; a small bag to fill with leaves or moss for a pillow pays for itself in one night. Flannel or woolen clothing, with roomy boots and a soft felt hat, is ordinarily the safest dress. Ladies, wear what you have a mind to, you will, anyway—but let it be flannel next to you, good strong shoes under foot, and a man's felt hat overhead ; take the man along, too—he will be useful to take the fish off your hook, run errands, etc.

"Boats and provisions may be obtained at almost any of the hotels. Bacon, salt pork, bread and butter, Boston crackers, tea, coffee, sugar, pepper and salt, with a tin box or two for containing the same, are among the things needed. Milk can be obtained regularly at the farm houses, and berries picked almost anywhere. Ice is a luxury which may be contracted for and thrown from the passing steamers daily ; a hole in the ground with a piece of bark over it forms a very good ice-box. A drinking cup of leather, to carry in the pocket comes handy at times. Broad-brimmed straw hats are a nuisance. A shanty of boughs will answer in absence of anything better ; it sounds well when you talk about 'roughing it,' but is bad in practice. A tent is best and may be made very comfortable with a little outlay of money and labor."

THE ADIRONDACKS.

The great wilderness of northeastern New York, the limits of which we will not try to define, is generally known as the North Woods, or as the Adirondacks, according to the view taken of its surface. The former title indicates merely a wild, densely wooded region ; the latter, a region occupied by all the varied scenery pertaining to a most remarkable lake and mountain system. This wild region of dense forest, majestic mountains, magnificent lakes and beautiful rivers, lies in the counties of Herkimer, Hamilton, Lewis, St. Lawrence, Clinton, Franklin and Essex, and aggregates over 3,500,000 acres, a tract of land of an area of nearly 100 square miles. This region is the only primitive hunting and fishing grounds left in New York State, and offering, as it does, rare health-restoring qualities combined with excellent deer hunting, and the best of brook and lake trout fishing accessible, is yearly more than doubling its number of visitors—in fact, the limit is only measured by hotel capacity. It is not our purpose, nor would it be possible in so small a work as this, to go into details as to the wilderness, but guide books are easily obtained, and The Delaware & Hudson R. R., issues a large amount of information upon the subject, which is easily obtainable from their General Passenger Agent, J. W. Burdick, Albany N. Y.

MY TRIP OVER THE GRAVITY RAILROAD.

In 1876, the centennial year, this country was visited by scores, yes, hundreds, of foreign visitors who came to our shores in quest of sights. Up to this time the company owning and working the Gravity railroad persistently refused any one transportation over it. No matter how much they pleaded or petitioned there was not anything they could do to move the heart of that corporation. At last light came through the darkness ; a female lawyer conceived the idea that way back in 1813, when the road was first built, the right of way was given as a public highway, and so she demanded transportation or they must abide the consequences.

I have been a great traveler in my day and have seen almost everything on this continent that is worth seeing. I was annoyed more by people asking questions about the Gravity railroad than as to any other spot in the country, so to the end that I might be in a better position to talk of it, I concluded to make the trip and see its beauties. Knowing that misery loves company,

I determined to take my daughter along, to the end that she could have the misery while I would be in good company.

We left Albany, N. Y., on Wednesday morning at 8.30 o'clock, over the Delaware and Hudson Canal Company's railroad. Station after station was passed; our eyes feasting upon the beauties of the mountain, valley, river, hillside and plain, but we had left that most beautiful of all pictures, Lake George, so could not drink in the ever changing scenes as we otherwise would. We were almost in dream land when a party of hop pickers boarded the train ; a happier, jollier, good natured crowd of country girls and boys we never saw before. The usual violin, guitar, bones and mouth organ accompanied them, and while they were with us, which was for over an hour, they kept up a continual revelry.

In the beautiful agricultural districts through which we passed, the corn fields were almost a bright yellow with the thousands of pumpkins that almost hid the earth from view. Our thoughts went back to the days when we were boys and made hideous jack lanterns to frighten nervous females and timid boys. One passenger remarked to another, " Is the pumpkin a berry or a fruit?" After a little discussion it was left to me, and I decided that it made berry good pie to say the least.

Can't say what struck the train ; the effect of that joke, probably, was the cause of the train coming to a standstill and suddenly the brakeman called out "Nineveh Junction, change cars," which we did, and were soon on our way to Carbondale, running under that greatest of stone viaducts, over which passes the Erie Railroad, and came to numerous coal pits, coal shafts and coal towns, and soon that long-looked-for announcement by the trainman breaks upon our eardrum, "Carbondale, change for the Gravity Railroad. This we did very quickly, and found we were noticed by a fine looking old gentleman we discovered to be the Superintendent, Mr. R. Manville. After looking us over for size, style and general appearance, he took us for some one of note, which we were, and ordered out an elegant new coach for our sole use, as there was not room in the regular. This was one occasion in my life that my weight and size helped me to gain a prominent position.

"All aboard," was the next sound I heard and looked around to see if I was all there, and we started. Our coach being in front, we acted as engine, and soon rounded at the first incline. Up to this time no propelling power was used, simply our weight and the gravity of the roadbed. Now we were attached to a cable and taken at the rate of ten or fifteen miles an hour up an incline; then a little way of our own gravity, we came to another incline, and so on to incline after incline, until we arrived at Far View, the top of a mountain 2,350 feet above the level of the sea. From that point we struck at what is called the ten mile lev but it has forty feet fall to the mile. And here we glide without any apparent power thirty or forty mi es per hour; without the annoyance of the engine, with its whistle, dust, smoke, and cinders, and so elated v'th our ride that we deem heaven but a little way off ; this huge body of mine was for a moment ethereal, imagining that I had been flying instead of the train.

Looking a little ahead I saw the village of Honesdale in the distance and a most magnificent hotel located on the top of a mountain or bluff in the rear of the village, and almost as quick as thought we arrived. Alighting from the car we were met by Mr. H. J. Conger, who took us in charge and escorted us to the Allen House. After a little preparation supper was announced, and if ever that word was appreciated it was on that occasion by myself as well as my daughter. After doing ample justice to that ever memorable meal, I was invited by Mr. Conger, and a lady guest at the hotel invited my daughter, to take a walk, as they desired to show us the village. It was on a Wednesday evening and all the different churches were sending forth their peal of the bell for the assembling together of the different congregations. Mr. Conger and myself were in deep conversation and did not notice we were holding the crowd behind us at bay by our slow martial tread. Presently I heard a remark coming from a lady directly behind us to this effect : " Who is that large, fleshy gentleman with Mr. Conger?" "I don't know, he must be a stranger in town." "Oh, I am sorry, I wish he lived here." "Why?" "If he did I would form his acquaintance very quickly and invite him up to the house every evening, six times a week." "What for?" "So he could sit down on our Bible and press our autumn leaves."

At this juncture we smiled and turned the corner, and proceeded up as far as the river bridge, then joining the ladies we passed through the principal business streets and returned to the hotel, after an hour and a half's walk. We parted with Mr. Conger, after spending a very pleasant hour in the parlor of the hotel with some of the guests, when our watch denoted the hour of bedtime had arrived. We retired * * * awoke if not with the lark, we "got there just the same," and about seven o'clock went to the depot to take the car, where we were introduced to Mr. William Muir, the superintendent of the Delaware & Hudson Canal Company at this point, who very kindly showed us the manner in which the cars were loaded with coal; also the different screens used in selecting the different sizes of coal and the manner in which that commodity is placed on canal boats. We also saw the working of the steam shovel in loading from huge mountains of coal.

At the time appointed we took our special car and proceeded to return to Carbondale. The distance from Carbondale to Honesdale is 16 miles, from Honesdale to Carbondale is 20 miles. Entering our car we arrive at the first incline, and were soon at that part of the road called Horseshoe Bend. This gorge was formerly spanned by a bridge 175 feet high. By gravity we pass around a curve. The sight of the autumn foliage is grand, and the beautiful little village of Seelyville in the distance. We arrive at incline number fourteen; there are twenty-eight of these inclines in all. The sight of the track below, one hundred cars loaded with coal, taking their serpentine windings around the various curves, run by an invisible power, is a sight once seen, never forgotten. Prompton Pass is the next place of note and we arrive at incline number sixteen, the engineer of which has made a beautiful flower garden amid rocks and coal which is very delightful to the eye. The large pond and station next in order is the feeder of the Delaware and Hudson canal. Waymart is the next station where trains are loaded, fifty cars each; this place is 1,450 feet above tide water. Next is incline number nineteen, over a half a mile in length, on the top of which is Far View, where we were met by Mr. R. Manville, who invited us to take a ride in his democrat wagon with two spirited horses attached. Had the wagon been any smaller or the horses any less, we would not have had the pleasure of taking in Far View. After they had procured a derrick and some steps I was gently raised into the seat in the vehicle and we proceeded on our tour of inspection. Everything that can be done, until the ingenuity of man is taxed to its utmost capacity for the pleasure and accommodation of visitors, has been done by the company. Hundreds of seats, chairs and benches are arranged everywhere.

Observatories, where you can ascend 150 feet to enhance your view ; grounds for base ball, croquet, lawn tennis ; in fact, everything to make it pleasant for picnic excursions or tourist travel has been done. We proceeded to the highest observatory, which we found was a little too high for our observation on account of a dense fog, so that we had to feast our eyes from below. The observatory is twenty-six hundred feet above the level of the sea, and from its summit may be seen nineteen small lakes or bodies of water, springs as it were, upon the top of the mountain. From one the company use twenty-six thousand gallons of water daily. A magnificent view of the Adirondacks of New York, the White Mountains of New Hampshire and Green Mountains of Vermont, can be had on a clear day. There is some talk of building a hotel here for tourists, of which, when completed, I want to be one of the first guests. The time having arrived to depart, we were invited to inspect the huge engine, boilers and fan wheel, used to convey cars up and down the incline, and we should advise visitors to take in the Engineers' art gallery, which is really a curiosity. Our car being attached to the regular train we proceeded on our way to Carbondale, which is twelve miles. Again on our way three miles and a half we are at the Shepherd's Crook. The engineer, conductor and brakeman are in one person, occupying the front platform. He put on the brake and our car stood still and we had the pleasure of seeing the regular train ahead pass around the Shepherd's Crook. After witnessing that novel sight, Mr. Manville told his brakeman to catch the regular train, which seemed to us about three miles ahead. All he had to do was simply to let up on his brake, and it seems as if we were there, for while I was taking in the scenes which greeted my eye we had joined the regular train, and I asked him how long before we would catch up to it, and I was informed we were already coupled on ; " for," said he, "the cows for the whole village of Carbondale pasture upon this hillside, and we have them educated for all the regular trains but not for specials, and for that reason I didn't care to run over any of the cattle and be accessory after the fact of their demise, so we coupled on to save trouble and expense." Looking out I saw a woman in charge of about eight or ten cows, and truthfully she was the homeliest person I ever saw. I asked him if they had female herderess here, and he remarked "yes." I then said they must use that one's face to wean the calves by.

"Carbondale, change cars."

After bidding everybody good-bye we took our seat in the D. & H. Company's regular train for Albany, arriving at five o'clock and thirty minutes in the afternoon.

LAKE GEORGE.

Every American, or tourist, should see it at least once. It is the largest of the Adirondack chain, 346 feet above the sea, and 247 above Champlain, thirty-five miles long and from two to four in width, and fed from mountain brooks and springs coming up from the bottom, making it transparent. It is beautifully dotted with over 200 islands, and surrounded by high mountains, some rising 2,000 feet above the water, clothed with foliage and dotted with villas and picturesque camps; one feels like leaving the boat and remaining in this bower of enchantment. The steamers touch at all points of note, and arrive at the Sagamore Hotel, where you can, if you desire, remain over.

THE SAGAMORE

stands among the trees at the south end of the Green Island, 40 feet above the level of the Lake, commanding from its upper windows the grand scenery of the Narrows on the east, the broad lake and bays at the south and west, and the mountains on every side.

The buildings comprising the Sagamore are of uncertain number, of varying levels, and picturesque in their grouping. The style is that popularly supposed to belong to the sixteenth century,—rising one back of another, with short flights of steps between, connected by open corridors with charming outlooks; its varied porticos, balconies and gables admirably displayed in colors that harmonize richly with their native surroundings.

Its interior finish is plain, but rich and substantial, showing massive beams, fireplaces of artistic designs in terra cotta, tinted walls and joiner work in native wood.

The furnishing is all that can be desired ; chairs and sofas, multiform and inviting, of different woods, polished and of willow ware ; the upholstery bright and cheerful ; the beds of the best kind procurable ; in short, no effort has been spared nor cost considered in making this the ideal hotel.

The main hall and office, and the principal parlor and reading and smoking rooms are on the main floor, looking out upon a semi-circular lawn, with flower bordered walks, leading down to the steamboat landing, and revealing between its stately trees delightful vistas of lake and islands beyond.

In the office are electric bells, with a system of wires running to the various rooms, placing them in immediate communication with base of supplies.

Telegraphic connection is made with the Western Union system at Caldwell by special wire in the office.

The news and notion stand supplies daily papers, periodicals, guides, maps, photographs, fine candles and fancy goods.

An elevator is here for the service of such as may prefer it to the short flight of steps by which the upper floors are reached.

The Edison incandescent Light is used throughout the entire establishment.

Spring water is brought from the mountains two miles away and 500 feet above the lake, and carried to every floor, where hose and pipe attachment affords the best of protection against possible danger from fire.

The sleeping rooms are spacious—many of them en suite, with private balconies and outside as well as hall entrances.

The sanitary conditions are perfect, made so by the

**IMAGE EVALUATION
TEST TARGET (MT-3)**

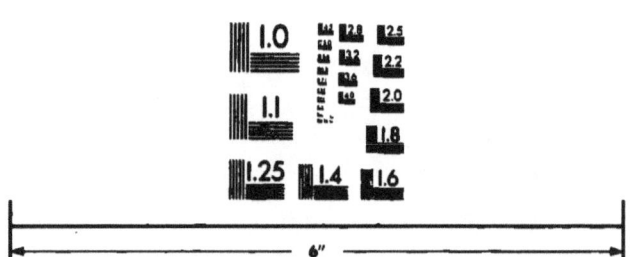

|←——————— 6" ———————→|

Photographic
Sciences
Corporation

23 WEST MAIN STREET
WEBSTER, N.Y. 14580
(716) 872-4503

employment of the most approved methods of drainage, for the application of which the location is admirably adapted.

Baths, hot and cold, may be had at the hotel and bath-houses outside ; while those who like open air and water for the sport, will find retired places and sandy beach near by.

Amusements : billiards and bowling within, and croquet, tennis, polo and archery without.

Riding and driving are provided for in the extensive stables on the island, and accommodations for those who may bring their own equipage. The drives are many and delightful.

Fishing, rowing, sailing or "steaming" are all made attractive by respectful attendants, and a fleet of boats ranging from the tiny skiff to the comfortable steam yacht.

A large hall for music and social gatherings has been built, connected with the main building at its highest point. Two new cottages also, and twenty-six new and desirable sleeping rooms have been added.

The line steamers land on every regular trip through the lake, connecting with the trains at each end, and run from Caldwell to the Sagamore dock on the arrival of the evening train from the south.

The proprietor, Mr. M. O. Brown, long and popularly known as a hotel man on the lake, will spare no pains to make your sojourn attractive in all respects.

The cuisine is perfect. The *Chef* and assistants are from the leading New York hotels. The head waiter, with his excellent and full corps of carefully trained and experienced waiters, the best that could be obtained.

As I have cheerfully recommended tourists for the last seven years to make a short stay at least at this delightful resort, the Sagamore (it is as near Heaven as many mortals will reach), get within its portals, if but for a short time, that you may realize its beauties, then you can thank me for the suggestion, as many others have, and I will be well repaid. Connections are, however, arranged for, and you can if you wish, leave immediately for Caldwell.

FACILITIES FOR LAKE TRAVEL.

The Champlain Transportation Company run a regular line of steamboats the entire length of the lake, making three round trips daily (except Sunday), and stopping at all way landings. The "Horicon" of this line, making the regular connections with the railroad, is a fine side-wheel steamer 203 feet long and 52 feet wide over all, and is 643 tons burden, and will accommodate comfortably 1,000 people. I can truthfully say that upon no inland lake in the world is the passenger service so promptly and regularly done, and passengers so elegantly cared for as upon Lake George.

Caldwell is the railroad terminus, and is the largest town on the lake. It is situated at the extreme southern end, or head of the lake (the waters flowing north and emptying into Lake Champlain, immediately at the ruins of old Fort Ticonderoga). At Caldwell is located the handsome dock and station building of the railroad company, whose trains run down the dock immediately to the steamers—one of which leaves upon the arrival of each train, for all points down the lake. The railroad was extended to this point in

1883, thus saving at least one hour of time, and better facilities for the accommodation of tourists and pleasure travel. The Adirondack R. R. has been purchased by the D. & H. Co., and hereafter will be known as the Adirondack Division of the D. & H. system.

SARATOGA SPRINGS,

the focus to which the fashionable world of the United States, indeed, of Europe, is annually drawn. Here are intellectual men, stylish men, the beaux of society, and the man of the world; ladies of social rank, the managing mother, the marriageable daughters, the fluttering bee of fashion, and the more gentle bird of beauty, are found amidst the throng, for Saratoga is cosmopolitan As a gentleman said to me one day, " I can meet more of my friends in one hour during the season at Saratoga than I could at home in a week." The ladies here have ample opportunities to display their peculiar charms and graces. The sporting gentleman can also find an opportunity to gratify his peculiar tastes; the philosopher may study human nature; the invalid find perfect health; in fact every one at Saratoga finds that peculiar pleasure they most desire. Of all the elegant hotels which here abound we have not space to mention. I will, therefore, speak of those that I know, the United States and the Adelphi, confident they can please any one paying them a visit.

THE UNITED STATES HOTEL, SARATOGA SPRINGS.

That magnificent Saratoga Palace, the United States Hotel, will open the present season on June 25th, and entertain many of the world's most distinguished people until October 1st next. Messrs. Tompkins, Gage & Perry, the proprietors, form a trio whose reputation as hotel men is not excelled anywhere. During the season each gives his personal attention to a department of the hotel, even to the minutest detail, and the result is, that their concert of action has won for them fame and fortune. Workmen are employed throughout the year. Every winter the plumbing, furniture, in fact everything in the interior of the hotel, is thoroughly examined by the corps of competent men who repair and improve where necessary, and each spring the exterior of the building, and park, walks, fountains etc., receive the same careful attention. Just now the outside of the hotel is being repainted. "Apropos" of this, a visitor said to me as we watched the painters industriously applying the paint, "Why, it seems almost a waste of money to paint that hotel this year, as it scarcely seems necessary;" and then he added, "Everything must be the pink of neatness and perfection about that hotel." He was right, and struck the key note of the policy adopted by those successful hotel proprietors. One of the most notable features of this hotel is the service. Even the hypercritical guest cannot find a loophole in this department through which to make a complaint. Each succeeding season, with but few exceptions, occasioned, perhaps, by sickness or death, the same competent staff returns to take up their old duties. I met Mr. Hiram Tompkins and Dr. Perry, who had just returned from New York, and they said, "The prospects of the season are excellent. We have already rented over two-thirds of our cottages for the summer, which to this date is without parallel in the past; of all the departments of the hotel the same can be said. Yes! Stub's Orchestra will return, and about all of the old help." But little if anything can be said here to add luster to this world-famed hotel. Make it your home while in Saratoga and you will have the satisfaction and consolation that no other hotel can give.

Next comes the Adelphi Hotel—this new, comfortable and petite hotel is located on Broadway, contains over one hundred rooms, is convenient to the springs, etc., etc. Its piazza is elevated one story above the street and commands a splendid view up and down Broadway, as well as Phila street, opposite. The proprietors, Messrs. Hayes and Brushnihan, are too well known to the traveling community to need one word from me, and the gentlemen connected with the office are of their own selection, and as they are young, like the proprietors, and brimming full of hotel business, and attend to the every want of their guests, you need not fear but you will be well cared for at the Adelphi. It is "my home" when in Saratoga; that is all I have to say against it. Under the Adelphi Hotel is the office of the Saratoga Kissengen Company. The Kissengen is "The King" of table waters. Drop in and examine its qualities; I feel confident you will be pleased. It is the universal opinion of tourist that no watering place on the continent, of like size, can compare with the unwearying charms of Saratoga. The hotel arrivals some days are upwards of one thousand. One might become almost tired of the world and vote every other place a bore, but Saratoga scenery, Saratoga atmosphere and Saratoga life would still charm by its ever pleasing peculiarities.

Mount McGregor, the place selected above all others for its pure air, etc., etc., as a residence for our hero,

Gen. U. S. Grant, who arrived at Saratoga on June 16th, 1885 (during my stay for health), so I had the pleasure of seeing the old veteran while he was being conveyed to the Mount McGregor R. R., which ascends to the top of the mountain, where visitors can go almost every hour and get a view that will well repay them. I left Saratoga on the morning of the 19th of June, and was informed by the conductor of the Mt. McGregor R. R., that General Grant rested well the previous night and slept ten hours. As all are aware, our hero departed this life July 23d. The cottage, however, is kept in the same manner as the day he left it, and will become an historic place for visitors who come to Saratoga from all parts of the world.

It is a fact, and worthy of note here, that for the past four years there has not been one day during the months of July and August, but they have had a heavy frost on Mount McGregor. I can vouch for the truthfulness of this item because I know him. He is the conductor of the train on the Mt. McGregor R. R., weighs 280 pounds, and his name is Frost. (He was a broad-gauge conductor on a narrow-gauge railroad.) Mr. Frost having accepted the agency for one of Saratoga's celebrated springs, there will not be a heavy frost on Mt. McGregor this year. He will be mist; won't his 280 pounds almost make a rain?

Saratoga contains 10,000 inhabitants and in the summer season every private house is turned into a boarding house of one or the other class, and therefore boarding houses abound—no space to mention all of them here.

Next in order comes the Springs, Congress and Hathorn.

EXCELSIOR SPRINGS AND PARK,

some distance from town, as well as others I shall mention, you can visit when you take a drive. Washington Spring is on the grounds of one of the hotels. Crystal, Pavilion, High Rock, Star, Seltzer, Red, A Spring, Geyser or spouting spring, Robert Ellis, The Vichy, "The Champion Spouting Spring," Hamilton, Putnam, Flat Rock, Magnetic, Sulphur, Iron, Diamond, Kissengen and Patterson, as well as a number of others which have been discovered or may have been before this reaches you. If, however, you are not satisfied with the springs herein mentioned, all I ask is for you to visit the ones mentioned, as I did, and accept the cordial invitation of each to take a glass, and if you do not feel the next day that there are springs enough at Saratoga, your feelings will be different from the sensations felt by the writer of this article, by a large majority. The drives in this vicinity are numerous. The road to the cemetery (which, I am informed by the oldest inhabitant, in order to start, they were obliged to borrow a corpse from an adjoining county, and now a select few who wish to die happy come and are decently interred), has been improved, so that the drive is very much enhanced thereby. By far the prettiest drive, however, is through Broadway from Highland Hill for two miles to Glen Mitchell. The most fashionable drive is that to the Lake. Immense sums of money have been expended to widen and beautify this drive, which is 100 feet wide and shaded with trees, and is sprinkled to lay the dust. Visitors pass up one side and down the other. Saratoga Lake is eight miles long and two and one-half wide. On an eminence on the western shore is Moon's

Lake House, proverbial for its sumptuous game suppers. Parties fond of fishing or boating can enjoy this favorite pastime to their full extent. Mr. Moon retired some years ago, being succeeded by Messrs. Kinney and Foley. Its fitness for aquatic sports have been verified by the many events of that nature which have taken place on its placid waters since 1871, when the Ward Brothers vanquished two English crews selected from the best professional oarsmen of Great Britain Racing is the turf event of the year, and cannot be described here, only mentioned.

Life at Saratoga is twofold—Home and Hotel. The former is enjoyed by its citizens, who possess some of the most luxurious, refined and elegant houses to be found in the United States. Hotel or fashionable life is ephemeral in its nature, and, like the beautiful butterfly, its duration is short. In these few brief months. wealth, beauty, fashion and other ingredients not so desirable, intermingle, and amid the gay whirl and excitement of the ball room at night one is in a constant ecstacy. From his visit to the springs in the morning, promenades or drives in the afternoon, the music, lawn sociable and glittering fireworks at night one wonders what time there is for nature's balmy, sweet restorer—sleep. Anticipating your stay at Saratoga to have come to an end, you can depart for Albany any morning via Delaware & Hudson Canal Co.'s R. R., or West Shore R. R., which run solid trains to and from Saratoga to New York, and New York to Saratoga, Pullman Buffet Cars. Some having tickets to New York by rail or boat, day or night from Albany to Troy. The general offices of all railroads or steamboats and bureau of information is in the Adelphi Hotel Building, presided over by my genial friend, Mr. C. E. Andrews. I advise every one to take the Fall River Line to Boston. If you have tickets to Boston via Albany, all rail, take the Boston & Albany railroad, which is first-class.

NEW YORK.

To those visiting New York for the first time a few words of advice may not come amiss. I therefore suggest arriving, if possible, by daylight. Every one in the city minds their own business—a credit in some ways; but some people make it their business to fleece the stranger. I would therefore say, keep your own counsel. If information be required ask a policeman. Upon arrival, take cars or cab, if possible to destination. If you desire any of the hotels represented in this work, you will always find one or more trusty porters at trains or boats. Avoid, if possible, the hacks, unless you make a fair, square bargain before entering the vehicle; your trunk or valise may accompany you with carriage. You will always find upon all trains or boats, courteous agents of the different baggage and express companies, who will take your check, giving a receipt for the same, which relieves you and saves you much trouble and annoyance, as their delivery system is prompt and their charges a stipulated price; no deviation, except for quantity.

Something should be said here regarding the metropolis of the American Continent, but space as well as time prevents. As everything seen here is in grandeur superior to elsewhere, the impression made upon the mind while here will be everlasting. I shall not try to befog the mind with as meagre a mention as I am capable of giving, but simply refer to the principal hotels. The first one at hand is the Grand Union Hotel, 42nd street, near the Grand Central Station. Money-getting being the chief aim of life, its proper expenditure should not prove of secondary importance. That travel consumes a much larger portion of our finances than it should, is evident from the fact that but a few possess the secret of retrenching in that direction. Two important factors of expense in travel are carriage hire and transfer of baggage ; and that the traveling public is more generally becoming disposed to throw off their former burden, is patent from the army of guests who daily register at and fill the 600 rooms (reduced to $1.00 and upwards per day) at the Grand Union Hotel, opposite the Grand Central Station, New York City. Its European plan, elegant restaurants, cafe, lunch and wine rooms, unexcelled cuisine, moderate prices, courteous treatment, unchallenged management, coupled with its guests incurring no expense for carriage hire or baggage transfer, with elevated railway, horse cars and cabs to all parts of the city passing its doors, render the Grand Union one of the most desirable, of homes for travelers in the city, and also established its success and world-famed popularity.

PLAZA HOTEL.

Fifth Avenue entrance Central Park.

While announcing the completion of one of the most perfect achievements of hotel art in modern times, and its formal opening on October 1st, 1890, it is appropriate to call especial attention to its peculiar advantages as a delightful residence for families and a convenient central and accessible resort for the transient tourist or business visitor to the city.

Situated at the centre of city population, on the block between 58th and 59th streets, fronting on Central Park and 5th Avenue Plaza, it commands charming views of both.

The location is unexceptionable, being accessible by 5th Avenue stages, 59th street cross and belt lines, passing steamship docks and all ferries elevated and surface railroads in the city, within half a block of the 6th Avenue elevated station where trains are made up always ensuring a seat down town.

Its proximity to the park affords unequaled advantage for riding and driving as no rough pavements intervene.

The building is absolutely fire proof and thoroughly lighted and ventilated. Every sanitary regulation and every modern improvement in electric and hydraulic arts to ensure the comfort, safety and convenience of guests are supplied in each department at a lavish expense. The culinary and domestic arrangement are models of modern attainment.

The furniture and appointments by the most celebrated makers are of the class used in the finest private residences, while the decorations of the public and private rooms are not surpassed in ornate elegance and artistic taste by any hotel in existence.

HYGEINA—The Plaza Hotel uses water and ice, made from vapor, thus avoiding all chance of disease from that source.

The evaporating apparatus and ice machine can be seen working on the premises at any time.

Superior arrangements are made for conducting the hotel on what are known as the American and European plans.

Office staff : Henry W. Riddell, Thomas W. Adams,

formerly of Windsor Hotel, N. Y. Jesse Hipple, formerly of Murray Hill Hotel, N. Y. Ira A. Swan, formerly of U. S. Hotel, Saratoga Springs.

Inspection is earnestly requested and letters of inquiry will receive prompt attention, address F. A. HAMMOND, Plaza Hotel, 5th Ave. & 59th St., New York.

A MAGNIFICENT HOTEL.

The Murray Hill Hotel is situated on Park Avenue in New York City, but one block from the Grand Central Station. A more convenient hotel site for the accommodation of the newly arrived traveler who would at the earliest moment find a home, could not have been selected. The house stands upon the highest grade in New York, and, of course, occupies the healthiest of locations. It is of great size, extending two hundred feet on the Avenue, more than two hundred feet on Fortieth street, on the one side, and Forty-first street on the other. It is of granite, brown stone and brick, fire-proof. When the traveler finds a hotel in every way meeting his demand for his comfort, he may honestly praise it while he disparages no other. For New York contains many costly structures, whose proprietors severally believe that their guests have reason to be satisfied. Hotels are not advertised as second class by those, that manage them. The man who is used to comfort at home is perhaps as good a judge as any one concerning what constitutes a satisfactory hotel. But, if you come to New York in the summer, I recommend you to this house, for in all this city there can be no healthier place in the warm season. There is a satisfaction felt at once upon entrance to this beautiful house. The vestibule is apparently just large enough ; the handsome, short flight of marble steps that lead to the office seem to be just long enough, the great hall seems just high enough to satisfy fully the idea that one has of proper architectural proportion. The floor is of marble, but not the hideous black and white inset diagonal. The Sienna is set against the slate and is a carpet pattern. One rather expects it to be soft and yielding to the foot, it looks so like a Wilton. The office is roomy ; not three or four only, but forty people may range themselves along its handsome counter ready to sign, in regular order, the register. The bookstand is no contracted affair, but space enough is given to allow display of, and easy access to, all periodicals and newspapers. Everything is on a grand scale, but altogether convenient. The great fire-place, which, with its burning logs, in winter invites the guest to share its comfort, is an attraction that merits and receives enthusiastic comment. The electric clock, lighted at night, the chandeliers, which at the proper time, because of the light touch of a knob somewhere, instantly illuminate halls and parlors, have their supply of electricity from the great machines in the basement, and the ice that is used for any purpose through all the house is made in huge condensers there. All the departments seem to be at all times in the best working order. All the employees seem ever willing to do their best to please the guest. There is a painstaking to furnish information when it is ask ed ; if one clerk does not know he directs you to one who does. In the matter of meals, they are ready at all hours. At the time of registry, the choice is made between the American and European plan, but the restaurants above and below stairs are always available. It would be easy for me to compliment the management and the efficient office staff, but that goes for the saying. As space is limited, I need only advise you to give the Murray Hill Hotel your patronage once ; they will see that you make it your home thereafter.

The hotel formerly called Grand Central Hotel, Broadway, is now the Broadway Central Hotel, and is under the management of Mr. Tilly Haynes, of the United States Hotel, Boston, Mass. It will be open this year on the first of July. Under the new management it has been refitted, redecorated and refurnished throughout.

greet the eye of an afflicted one, I feel positive after calling and being treated they would look upon me as a benefactor as long as they live for putting in my book this gratuitous notice. I received in April last from him a very neat pamphlet descriptive of cancers, their treatment and cure, which will be sent you free, pro-

come to New York in the summer, I recommend you to
this house, for in all this city there can be no healthier
place in the warm season. There is a satisfaction felt
at once upon entrance to this beautiful house. The
vestibule is apparently just large enough; the handsome, short flight of marble steps that lead to the office
seem to be just long enough, the great hall seems just
high enough to satisfy fully the idea that one has of
proper architectural proportion. The floor is of marble,
but not the hideous black and white inset diagonal.
The Sienna is set against the slate and is a carpet pattern. One rather expects it to be soft and yielding to
the foot, it looks so like a Wilton. The office is roomy;
not th   only but forty people may range
thems
in re
contr
displ
pape
conv
ing
is an
comment. The electric clock, lighted at night, the
chandeliers, which at the proper time, because of the
light touch of a knob somewhere, instantly illuminate
halls and parlors, have their supply of electricity from
the great machines in the basement, and the ice that is
used for any purpose through all the house is made in

huge condensers there. All the departments seem to be at all times in the best working order. All the employees seem ever willing to do their best to please the guest. There is a painstaking to furnish information when it is asked ; if one clerk does not know he directs you to one who does. In the matter of meals, they are ready at all hours. At the time of registry, the choice is made between the American and European plan, but the restaurants above and below stairs are always available. It would be easy for me to compliment the management and the efficient office staff, but that goes for the saying. As space is limited, I need only advise you to give the Murray Hill Hotel your patronage once ; they will see that you make it your home thereafter.

While in New York, about the middle of June, I thought it would be a good idea if some one of the many merchants in the city were to advertise in this little volume ; knowing that it is not thrown away but retained as a souvenir, it will be a perpetual advertisement ; I called on Dr. W. L. Fleming, "The Cancer King," of "The Ariston," Broadway and 55th St., New York City, who showed me hundreds of cancers, which he removes without the aid of a knife. If this should greet the eye of an afflicted one, I feel positive after calling and being treated they would look upon me as a benefactor as long as they live for putting in my book this gratuitous notice. I received in April last from him a very neat pamphlet descriptive of cancers, their treatment and cure, which will be sent you free, provided you mention this book or its author. I also visited three of the leading dry goods firms. No. 1 stated that I was too late they did no summer business. No. 2 said my price was too high, but as I spend all the money I procure from advertisers on the printing of books and get my money off the sale, his point was not well taken. No. 3 invited me to call next season, which I hope to have the pleasure of doing. I would like to say here that I published this book and advised the advertisers therein to take the space, feeling it would bring back to them four-fold what they paid me. It will, therefore, afford me pleasure to have you mention to any of the advertisers that it was through my solicitation and this work that you favored them with your patronage; it will do you no harm and benefit me.

BOSTON

is one of the most interesting of American cities, not only on account of its thrilling traditions and historical associations, but for public enterprise and social culture, educational and literary facilities. Boston is peculiarly Boston, and no one can describe its public, private or natural beauties in the space allotted me here. The principal sights are Bunker Hill Monument, Faneuil Hall, the Common, Public Garden, Old and New State Houses, Public Library, Old and New South Churches, Natural History buildings, Agricultural buildings, Institute of Technology, New Trinity Church, Mount Auburn, Harvard University buildings, Music Hall, the Great Organ, City Hall, Hospitals and other sights too numerous to mention here. Trimountain, or Three Mountains, as Boston was originally called, is a peninsula of about 700 acres, almost surrounded by the sea. Its climate in the hottest part of seasons is deliciously cool, bracing and invigorating, and it is undoubtedly one of the healthiest cities in the world. Its harbor, one of the best on the coast, is about twenty miles long by eight wide. Its many islands and coasts are lined with thousands of delightful summer resorts, reached by numerous railroads and steamboats every hour of the day, forming a panorama of busy life and pleasure to be seen nowhere else. Its drives inland are none the less interesting and picturesque, whether we visit the classic shades of old Harvard, the romantic walks at Wellesley, or the hundred delightful suburban villages, whose well-kept streets, bright lawns and elegant gardens simply reflect the elegance and taste within the homes of those who have made Boston what it is. The excellent horse-car service of Boston is one of the best institutions. Nowhere else in the country is this important convenience to visitors so complete as here. The broad, handsome, open cars reach all points within ten miles of the City Hall, and give visitors a most delightful opportunity to see the attractions at the least possible charge.

Boston, the Capital of Massachusetts, embraces Boston proper, East Boston, South Boston, Roxbury, West Roxbury, Brighton, Charlestown and Dorchester. Boston proper, or old Boston, was very uneven in surface, and originally presenting three hills, Bacon, Copp's, the Fort, the former of which is about 130 feet above the sea. The Indian name of this peninsula was Shawmut, meaning "Sweet waters." A narrow strip of land called the "Neck" joined the peninsula to the main land ; this neck was formerly overflowed by the tide, but has been filled in and widened, and is now thickly built upon. East Boston occupies the west portion of Noodle's or Maverick's Island. Here is the deepest water of the harbor, and here the ocean steamers chiefly lie. The wharf now used by the Cunard steamers is 1,000 feet long. South Boston extends about two miles along the south side of the harbor, an arm of which separates it from Boston proper.

The first white inhabitant of Boston was the Rev. John Blackstone, supposed to have been an Episcopal clergyman, and to have arrived in 1623. Here he lived until 1630, when John Winthrop (afterward the first Governor of Massachusetts) came across the river from Charlestown, where he had dwelt with some fellow immigrants for a short time. About 1635 Mr. Blackstone sold his claim to the now populous peninsula for £30, and removed to Rhode Island. The first church was built in 1632; the first wharf in 1673. Four years later a postmaster was appointed, and in 1704 (April 24th), the first newspaper, called the *Boston News Letter*, was published. The "Boston Massacre" happened March 5, 1770, when three persons were killed and five wounded by the fire of the soldiers. In 1773 tea was destroyed in the harbor, and Boston bore a conspicuous part in the opening scenes of the Revolution. The city was incorporated in 1822, with a population of 45,000, which had increased to 136,881 in 1850, to 177,850 in 1860, and 250,526 in 1870. By the recent annexation of the suburbs of Brighton, Charlestown, West Roxbury, etc, the population has been increased to 341,919 (in February, 1876). Population 362,876 in 1880, and 448,447 in 1890. On the 9th of November, 1872, one of the most terrible conflagrations ever known in the United States swept away the principal business portion of Boston.

The fire broke out on Saturday evening, and continued until noon on the following day when it was brought under control, but again broke forth in consequence of an explosion of gas, about midnight, and raged until 7 o'clock Monday morning. The district burned over extended from Summer and Bedford street on the south, to near State street on the north, and from Washington street east to the harbor. About 800 of the finest buildings in the city were destroyed, causing a loss of $80,000,000.

OBJECTS OF ANTIQUARIAN INTEREST.

Among "buildings with a history," the most interesting in the United States, next to Independence Hall in Philadelphia, is Faneuil Hall. The famous edifice, the "cradle of liberty," is in Dock Square, which also has an historical fame, because of the meetings of the Revolutionary patriots that were held there. The building was erected in 1742, by Peter Faneuil, a Huguenot merchant, and by him presented to the town. Its original dimensions were 100 by 40 feet. Destroyed by fire in 1761, it was rebuilt in 1763, and enlarged to its present dimensions in 1805. A full length portrait of the founder, together with the pictures of Washington, by Stuart, of Webster, by Healy, of Samuel Adams, by Copely, and portraits of John Quincy Adams, Edward Everett, Abraham Lincoln and Governor Andrew adorn the walls. The basement of the hall is a market. The old State House, in Washington street, at the head of State street, was erected in 1748, and was for half a century the seat of the "Great and General Court of Massachusetts," being the building of which such frequent mention is made in revolutionary annals. It has long been given up to business purposes, the interior having been completely remodeled, and the edifice surrounded by a roof which has wholly destroyed the quaint effect of the original architecture. Christ Church (Episcopal), in Salem street, near Copp's Hill, is the oldest church in the city, having been erected in 1722. It has a lofty steeple, and in the tower is a fine chime of bells. The Old South Church, corner of Washington and Milk street, is an object of much interest. It is of brick, and was built in 1729, on the site where the first edifice of the society has stood from 1669. The church was used as a place of meeting by the heroes of '76, and during the British occupation of the city was used as a place for cavalry drill. It barely escaped the flames in the great fire. The Old South Society having erected a new place of worship on Boylston street, the old building was offered for sale, when a patriotic effort among the people originated a subscription for the purpose of raising funds to secure its preservation. King's Chapel (Unitarian), corner Tremont and School streets, was founded in 1686, and the present building, a plain granite structure, erected in 1750-54. Adjoining the church is the first burying-ground established in Boston. In it are buried Isaac Johnson, " the Father of Boston," Governor Winthrop, John Cotton and other distinguished men. On the corner of Washington and School streets is the Old Corner Book Store, a building dating from 1712. The Old North Burying-ground, on the brow of Copp's Hill, was the second established in the city, and is still sacredly preserved. Here lie three fathers of the Puritan Church, Drs. Increase, Cotton and Samuel Mather.

THE OLD CEMETERY IN THE COMMON.

In that corner of the Common bounded by Tremont and Boylston streets, and lying directly between the Masonic Temple and the Public Library, is an old burying-ground, shut off from the common and the streets by an iron fence. It was formerly known as the South, and later as the Central Burying ground. It was opened in 1756, but the oldest stone is dated 1761. The best known name upon any of the ancient stones is that of Monsieur Julien, the most noted *restauranteur* of the city a century past, and the inventor of the famous soap that still bears his name. This cemetery is the least interesting of the old burying places of Boston, and is consequently seldom noticed by the stranger.

There are, according to the directory, nearly two hundred hotels in the city. With that fact in view, I shall mention, first the United States. In suggesting to intending visitors to Boston the name of the

"UNITED STATES HOTEL,"

the proprietor feels satisfied in recommending the house for just what it is, no more, no less. I am at home when in the United States Hotel; it pleases me, and I am positive it will please you.

The United States Hotel is one of the oldest and best of the well-established hotels of Boston. Its fame is wide-spread. Its seal dates back to 1826, and from that early date to the present it has been maintained up to the best standard, but never better than now. It is situated directly opposite the Boston & Albany, within two blocks of the Old Colony, and only a short distance from the New York & New England, and Providence Railroad stations, and is the nearest hotel to the retail portion of the city and the great commercial centers.

The "United States" is occupied largely in winter by families owning their own private residences in the adjoining towns, who come into the city and make their residence at this famous old house for the winter months. During the summer season, therefore, their great family rooms are available for tourists, families and pleasure parties, giving accommodations that could not otherwise be afforded, and so allow guests the most extensive variety of rooms at the lowest possible charges. During the summer months the rates are reduced to $2.50, $3.00 and $3.50 per day, according to accommodations, with board; rooms without board $1.00 and upwards, thus giving visitors an opportunity of making this hotel their permanent headquarters, from which to make daily excursions to the thousand places of historical interest with which the city and suburbs abound, and to the great manufacturing cities which surround it; while the fifteen hundred summer resorts and boarding houses down the harbor and along the coast are available every fifteen minutes by boat or rail. Thus the "United States" will be found not only a most accessible and convenient hotel on arriving at Boston, but will be found equally comfortable and economical for permanent as well as transient guests, while the facilities for reaching all the suburban localities and various sea shore resorts are unequaled by any hotel in Boston.

My dear friend, John B. Schoeffel, will, I am glad to know, manage this year his summer home, "Manchester by the Sea," the finest resort on the coast. If you have time for only a call, take the Boston & Maine R. R., Gloucester branch, only 35 miles from Boston. It is the summer home of Agnes Booth, John Gilbert, Joseph Proctor, Mrs. Bowers, Franklin Haven, Pres. Merchants Bank, and a host of others. Beautiful harbor and beach bathing nine months in the year, drives unsurpassed in America; therefore if you are looking for the best in the land, visit Manchester by the Sea and be happy.

One of the best traveling companions on a pleasure trip is a reliable Railway Guide, and we advise the tourist to get the best, as a cheap guide is like a cheap watch—never on time.

As we hold that this little volume is not thrown away, but taken home for future reference, a little advice of how to start upon a trip, etc., would not come amiss. We say

1st, Select your route. 2d, Buy your tickets and secure your parlor car seats. 3d, show your tickets to the baggage master and have your baggage checked. 4th, Go to the news stand and ask for The "Phat Boy's" 18 years on the St. Lawrence, or the Pathfinder's Railway Guide as it is the oldest railway guide published, and the July number will contain the best railroad map ever published. It is the only recognized mouthpiece of the Passenger Agents' Association; one can be assured of its reliability. The Phat Boy requests his friends to send to them next spring for a copy of their summer 'ours to select your vacation trip. Address, Pathfinder, Boston, Mass. 5th, Don't bother the conductor by questions, as he has all he can do to attend to his train, and the Pathfinder's official tables and valuable maps tell the whole story.

I have endeavored to describe faithfully and correctly the route over which you have passed, dear reader. There are, doubtless, some whose knowledge of particular points is greater than my own; to those I say most cheerfully, note them down, and forward to me 21 Chestnut Park, Rochester, N. Y., and I assure you they shall have a position in the next edition of this work, as my object and aim is to make this a perfect guide for any person desirous of making this the finest trip on the continent.

While it has never been published, to my knowledge, it is a cold fact that Grover Cleveland paralyzed Dan Manning with ingratitude, and last June I received a dose of that commodity from the General Passenger Agent of the Boston & Lowell R R. that would have paralyzed Cleveland. Therefore I say to my friends, whenever you can avoid patronizing that railroad without injury to the Central Vermont, do so, and you will do me the greatest favor of a lifetime. This spring I was obliged to make my usual trip and visit all the advertising patrons in my books and maps. Meeting a friend who mentioned having read of the unkind treatment dealt out to me by the above railroad, suggested that I take a day off and study the railroad geography of the country and see if there was not some way around, that was just as sure to reach my destination. A happy thought, said I, and I was not long in determining to take the Fitchburg R. R. via Bellows Falls, or Windsor, Vermont, where I made connections and arrived in Montreal on time. Therefore, I say to my friends if you patronize the Fitchburg R. R. between Montreal & Boston, may you have as pleasant a journey as the subscriber and I know you will never regret it.

After returning home and resuming the cares and position which you left behind for this trip, may you be filled with animation, life and health acquired by your excursion trip down the St. Lawrence, etc., and the pleasant memories of scenes witnessed, wonders visited, as well as the beauties of nature revealed, you will have double the vigor to prosecute the duties devolving upon you, with only spare time on hand to speak to your acquaintances and friends, recommending them to make the same trip, not forgetting to mention The "Phat Boy's" 18 years on the St. Lawrence River as a guide for hotel and all points of interest connected with the trip. I will now lift my hat to the tourists and others who have made the trip, and bid them a temporary farewell. Hoping to see, next vacation, yourself and friends, I only say

ADIEU.

www.ingramcontent.com/pod-product-compliance
Lightning Source LLC
Chambersburg PA
CBHW020859230426
43666CB00008B/1240